# Baking Wonderland

It's Good, Eh?
Glaze
(page 117)

Stuff
(page 138)

Chocolate
Date Donut
(page 161)

Her Royal
Highness Icing
(page 118)

# BAKING WONDERLAND

## A Mix and Match Cookbook for Kids!

By Jean Parker and Rachel Smith

appetite
by RANDOM HOUSE

Appetite by Random House® and colophon are registered trademarks of Penguin Random House LLC.

Library and Archives of Canada Cataloging in Publication is available upon request.

ISBN: 978-0-525-61224-7
eBook ISBN: 978-0-525-61225-4

Photography by Reena Newman
Illustration by Angela Chao
Book design and additional illustration by Emma Dolan

Printed in China

Published in Canada by Appetite by Random House®, a division of Penguin Random House Canada Limited

www.penguinrandomhouse.ca

10 9 8 7 6 5 4 3 2 1

appetite
by RANDOM HOUSE

Penguin
Random House
Canada

For our mom,
our starting place.

Stuff
(page 138)

# Contents

Shoe-nuts Donuts
(page 154)

Chocolate
Shine Glaze
(page 121)

Buttercream
Bomb Frosting
(page 107)

Goldilocks's
Oatmeal Cookies
(page 53)

Her Royal
Highness Icing
(page 118)

Strawberry
Patch Frosting
(page 114)

Wonderland
Cookies
(page 41)

Baked
Strawberry and
Cream Donuts
(page 171)

Gingerbread
Molasses Cookies
(page 51)

Fluffy Cream
Cheese Frosting
(page 111)

# WELCOME
## ...•.. TO ..•...
# WONDERLAND

Are you ready for a baking adventure? Welcome to Baking Wonderland, the sweetest place on Earth!

Hi! We're sisters Jean and Rachel and we love to bake, so we've created a magical place full of delicious, easy-to-follow recipes for you to discover! Be our guest and explore our theme park full of the most scrumptious cookie, cupcake, donut and cake recipes. Mix and match them with our fabulous frostings, fillings, glazes, drizzles, toppings and drinks to build your dream dessert! There are over 300 combinations to try, and they all taste delicious!

Whether you start your adventure on our cookie carousel or take a spin on our cupcake Ferris wheel, we know you'll have fun and learn some cool and interesting stuff along the way! Just ask our animal friends from the carousel—if you can find them!

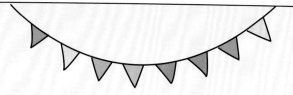

# How Does This Book Work?

This mix-and-match cookbook is for curious kids who love to laugh, use their imaginations and play with their food! If this sounds like you, you're in the right place! Have fun! Make something yummy. This is your cookbook and YOU decide what to bake.

## USE THE MAP

First, explore the map of our Baking Wonderland on the inside cover of this book! This big picture shows the types of recipes that are in this book and where to find them. Did you notice that our map has four delicious lands to visit? They're called Cookieland, Cupcakeland, Donutland and Cakeland! And did you spot our amazing Wonderpark? Wonderpark is where you'll find the recipes for our fillings, frostings, glazes, toppings, milks and more!

Start your baking adventure by looking at our map to decide which cookie, cupcake, donut or cake you'll bake today. Make sure to put a bookmark on the page so you can find the recipe easily!

## MIX AND MATCH!

Next, head to Wonderpark and choose a wonderful recipe to go with your dessert! Will you pick an ooey-gooey filling to go inside it? Or a fabulous frosting, a sticky glaze or a fun topping to go on top of it? Maybe you'll make a creamy drink to go on the side! Maybe you'll make them all! Whatever you decide, make sure to put a bookmark in these pages too!

## YAY! YOU'RE READY TO BAKE!

Follow each recipe one at a time. When you're done, put them together to build your dream dessert! We can't wait to see what awesome flavor combinations you come up with!

P.S. Don't forget to take a slip on our milk slides (page 140) before you go! It's udderly fun!

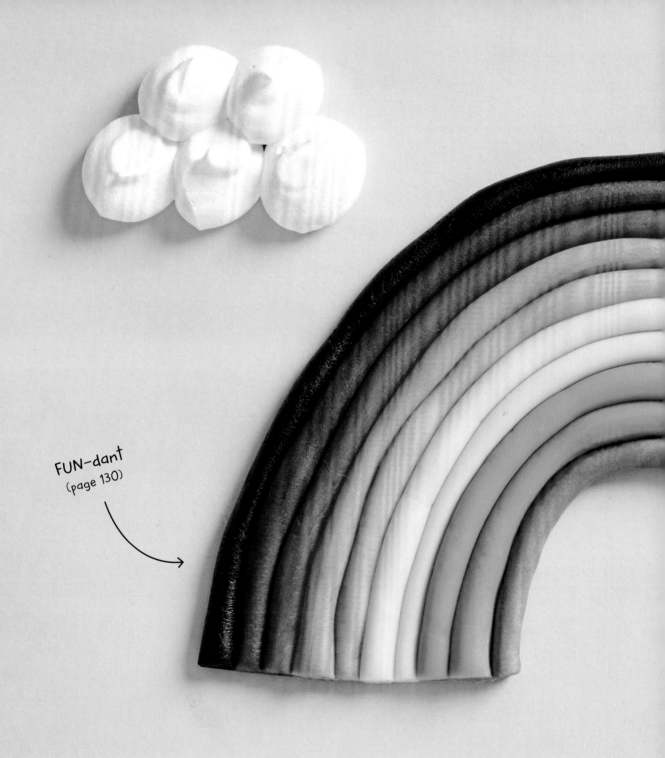

FUN-dant
(page 130)

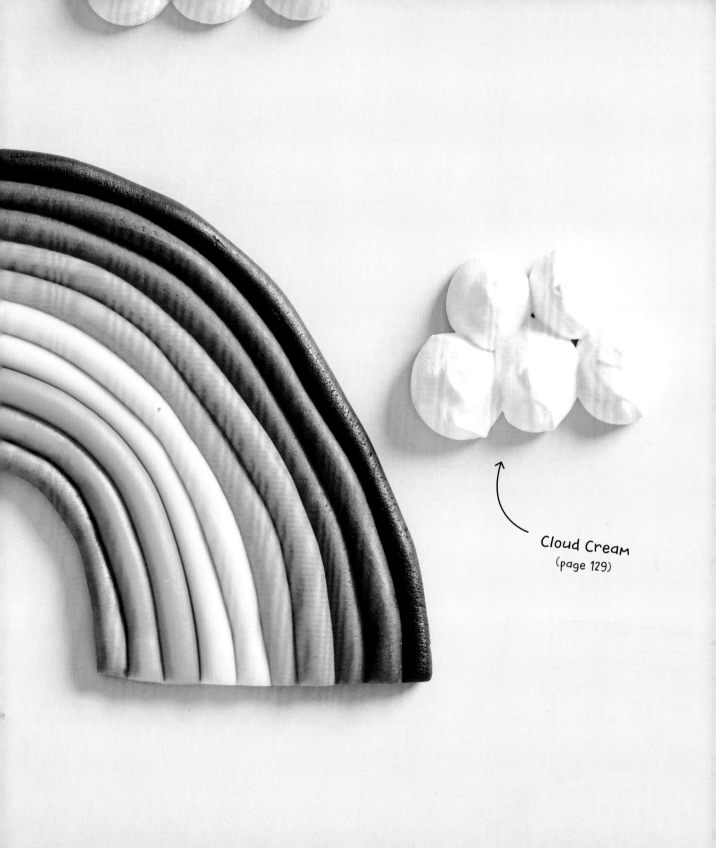

Cloud Cream
(page 129)

# INFORMATION BOOTH

Step right up! This area of Baking Wonderland is where you'll find oodles of information about baking. Start by meeting our Wonder Tools and discover their superpowers. Then visit our Measuring Table and learn about measuring ingredients, or stop by the Coloring Box to learn about how you can mix colors to create new ones. Whether you're sifting, piping, boiling or laughing, our Information Booth has the information you need to make your baking time a breeze!

# Reading the Recipes

To help guide you on your baking adventure, we've come up with some symbols. They're here to help you remember what to do. See below to find out what they mean, and have fun finding them in our recipes!

## GET READY!

This symbol tells you to get ready by gathering your tools and measuring your ingredients! It's super important to do this before you begin baking, as some recipes call for special tools and others call for special ingredients that you might not have met before. Once you've gathered everything and measured it all out, you can flip the page and begin your baking adventure. How fun!

## THERE'S MORE TO EXPLORE!

This symbol tells you there are more things to discover about the recipe. You'll find heaps more information in our Information Booth!

## THIS RECIPE NEEDS EGG-XTRA TIME!

This symbol tells you that this recipe takes a little more time to make—sometimes a few hours, and sometimes overnight, so plan ahead.

## FIND YOUR PERSON

(also known as a grown-up)

When you see this symbol, FIND YOUR PERSON to help you with the oven, stove or tricky bits in the recipe. We bet your person will also make a wonderful taste tester!

## YOUR IMAGINATION!

When you see this symbol, it's time to get creative and mix and match your recipes. Use your imagination to come up with fun flavor combinations and dreamy decorations. The possibilities are endless!

## YOUR CURIOSITY!

We've got a bunch of fun facts about baking for you. And that's a fact!

## YOUR SENSE OF HUMOR!

Baking should never be too serious. It's just dessert after all. Now get ready to laugh! Yolk yolk yolk!

## GLUTEN-FREE

Gluten is found in grains like wheat, rye and barley. When you see this symbol it means there is no gluten in the recipe.

## VEGAN

This symbol means that the recipe is made without any animal products, like milk or eggs.

## What does that mean?

There are also some short forms of words commonly used in baking that are good to know. Here's what they mean:

TSP = teaspoon

TBSP = tablespoon

OZ = ounce

°F = degrees Fahrenheit

°C = degrees Celsius

LOL = laugh out loud

Yolk yolk yolk! This book is egg-cellent!

# Wonder Tools

It's a spoon . . . it's a whisk . . . it's the Wonder Tools! These five great baking tools play an important role in baking. Each one has a special superpower and should be used a certain way. Here's who they are and what they do! Look out for these Wonder Tools in all the recipes!

## MIXING SPOON

When you see this spoon, it's time to MIX. To MIX means to slowly and gently stir your ingredients together. To do this, stick your spoon into your bowl and slowly move it around the bowl in a circle.

## WHISK

Any time you see this picture, it's time to WHISK. To WHISK, use your whisk just like you would use a mixing spoon but make smaller, quick circles or figure eights in the center of your bowl.

## SPATULA

Any time you see this picture of the spatula, it's time to SCRAPE or FOLD. To SCRAPE means to remove the batter from the sides and bottom of a bowl. To do this, run the edge of the spatula down the sides and bottom of the bowl, pushing any ingredients that might have been stuck back into the center.

To FOLD means to mix light airy ingredients with heavier ones. To do this, gently dip your spatula into the batter and lift the heavier ingredients at the bottom of the bowl to the top. The action is kinda like flipping a pancake and should be done very gently to keep your light ingredients nice and fluffy.

## ELECTRIC MIXER

Any time you see this lil' guy, it's time to BEAT your ingredients using an electric mixer. To BEAT means to mix the ingredients really, really fast, making your mixture smooth and airy.

### Here's how you do it:

1. Start by making sure the electric mixer is UNPLUGGED. Super!

2. Next, attach the beaters to the mixer. Excellent.

3. Make sure the dial is turned to the off position. Perfect.

4. Now plug in the electric mixer safely.

5. Hold onto the electric mixer with 1 hand, and firmly hold onto the bowl with the other.

6. Lower the beaters into the bowl.

7. Turn on the mixer to the lowest speed—always start on the lowest speed and then slowly turn it up if you need to. This will keep the ingredients from blasting off to outer space.

8. Now move the electric mixer around the bowl in a circle, doing your best to keep the beaters straight up and down. Yay! You're beating like a boss!

## YOUR HANDS

Your HANDS are the most important tool you've got! Look at them. Hold them up and take a real good look at them. Aren't they fantastic? They're incredible! Your hands will do all sorts of amazing things in your lifetime! In Baking Wonderland, they'll knead doughs, roll cookies and poke holes into cupcakes! How wonderful is that?

# Measuring Table

When it comes to baking, paying attention to how much of each ingredient to use in your recipe is super-duper important! Too much of something could make your baked good wiggle, plop or slide! Too little could make it flip, flop or deflate! So let's talk a little about measuring.

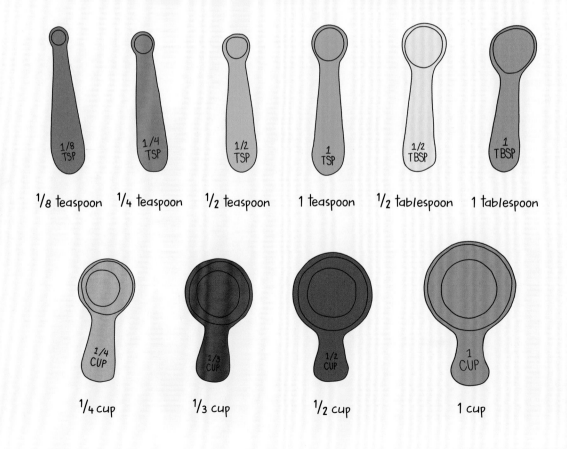

1/8 teaspoon   1/4 teaspoon   1/2 teaspoon   1 teaspoon   1/2 tablespoon   1 tablespoon

1/4 cup   1/3 cup   1/2 cup   1 cup

## DRY INGREDIENTS

To measure dry ingredients like cocoa powder, baking soda and salt, we use measuring cups and spoons. You can fill measuring cups and spoons up to the top with ingredients and then carefully take off any extra, to get the perfect amount every time.Measuring cups and spoons come in all sorts of sizes. To the left you'll see the sizes we use in our recipes.

## WET INGREDIENTS

We use liquid measuring cups for sloshy ingredients like oil, milk and water. They have measurements written along the side of the cup so you can add the ingredients up to the amount you need. They often have a spout and a handle, making pouring easy to do and spill-free!

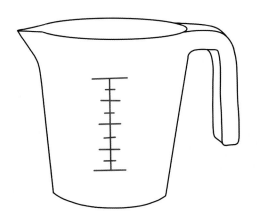

## THE SCOOP ON FLOUR AND BROWN SUGAR

Flour and brown sugar are two ingredients that need special attention when measuring: too much flour in your recipe will make your baking heavy and dense, too little brown sugar will make your recipe dry and bland. Here's how to get the best cup of each.

### Measuring flour? Here's how you do it:

1. Using a big spoon, spoon the flour into the measuring cup until it's overflowing and it looks like a tiny hill.

2. Now take a butter knife and scrape off the top of the tiny hill so the flour is even with the top of the cup.

3. Yay! You did it. A perfectly measured cup of flour.

### Measuring brown sugar? Here's how you do it:

1. Using a big spoon, spoon the brown sugar into the measuring cup until it's overflowing and looks like a tiny hill.

2. Now take your HANDS and press down on the sugar, packing it down flat. Keep adding more sugar and pressing down until the sugar is even with the top of the cup.

3. Yay! You did it. A perfectly measured cup of brown sugar.

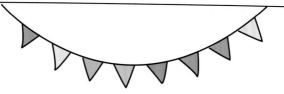

# Separating Eggs

An egg is an awesome ingredient to bake with! A whole egg is made up of an egg yolk (the yellow circle in the middle) and an egg white (the runny goo around the yolk). Egg yolks will keep your baking moist and rich in flavor, and egg whites will make your baking light and airy. And they both do a great job of holding all of the other ingredients you're baking with together! Sometimes a recipe will need just the yolk or just the egg white and you'll need to separate them from each other.

### Here's how you do it:

1. Place 2 bowls on the counter.

2. Crack the egg lightly on the countertop, just enough to break it.

3. Open the shell carefully while holding the egg over 1 of the bowls.

4. Gently pour the egg into the palm of your clean hand, catching the yolk in your fingers and allowing the whites to slowly slide through your fingers and into the bowl.

5. Place the yolk into the other bowl.

6. Yay! You did it. A perfectly separated egg.

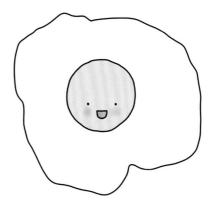

# Preparing Pans

Hey, bakers! There's nothing crummier than your delicious desserts sticking to your pans after baking. So here are the types of baking pans you'll use and our favorite ways to slick 'em so nothing sticks.

## COOKIE SHEETS

Silicone baking mats are awesome for lining your cookie sheets. The teeny-tiny bumps on the mat act as little grippers and keep the cookie dough from spreading during baking. If you don't have any mats, line each cookie sheet with a piece of parchment paper.

## MUFFIN PANS

For our cupcakes, we like to use cupcake liners AND cooking spray! Place 1 cupcake liner in each cup of the muffin pan and then lightly spray the whole pan with cooking spray. This will let the cupcake peel away easily from the liner when you're ready to eat it. How neat!

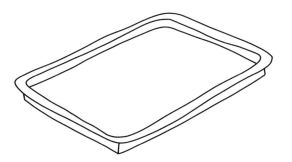

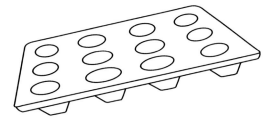

## CAKE PANS

We like to line the bottom of cake and loaf pans with parchment paper and then spray the whole thing with cooking spray.

To get the parchment paper to fit perfectly into round cake pans, start with a piece of parchment paper larger than the pan. Place the cake pan on top of the paper, right side up. Now take a pencil and trace around the bottom of the pan. You've just drawn a perfect circle! Grab some scissors and carefully cut out the circle. Do your best to cut along the line.

Place the parchment circle in the bottom of the pan and spray the whole inside of the pan with cooking spray, coating all of the sides. Make sure you remove the piece of parchment paper after your cake has baked and cooled!

## DONUT PANS

These 6-ring pans are perfect for baking donuts in, but batter can get stuck in their grooves. We like to slather each ring first in coconut oil AND lightly spray the whole thing with cooking spray before filling it with batter! First, take a pastry brush and generously dip it into coconut oil. Then, as if you're painting, paint the rings (don't forget the sides and tops) with coconut oil. Now, lightly spray the whole inside of the pan with cooking spray. Not only do the coconut oil and the cooking spray help release the donuts after baking but they also help them bake up a little crispy. Delish!

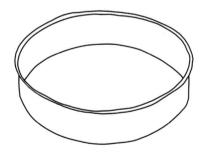

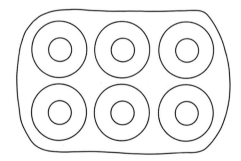

DON'T SHOOT! Before you begin spraying cooking spray, make sure the nozzle is facing the baking pan and about the length of a wiener dog away from the pan.

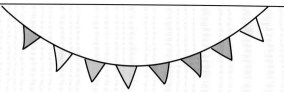

# The Whipped Peak

Whether you're whipping up a luscious filling or a velvety frosting, how long you BEAT your cream, sugar or eggs changes from recipe to recipe. Recipes often use the word "peak" to help you know when to stop beating. (The peak is the little mountain of ingredients on the beaters when you lift them out of the bowl.)

**Soft peak**: This little mountain barely stands up when you take the beaters out. The top of it will flop over right away. We use soft peaks to make our Vanilla Ice Scream (page 100).

**Medium peak**: This little mountain holds its shape when you lift the beaters out of the bowl but the top will curl over! These peaks are perfect for the whipped cream in our Princess Banana Lips filling (page 98).

**Stiff, firm or hard peak**: This little mountain of yum stands straight up when you pull the beaters out of the bowl. Stiff peaks are a must for our Poop Cookies (page 47).

# Everything You KNEAD to Know about KNEADING!

### What is kneading?

Kneading is the action of working dough with your hands by pulling, pushing and pressing it over and over again.

### Why do we need to knead?

Kneading makes the dough strong and elastic. That's important because the dough needs to hold up all of the bubbles made by the yeast inside it—this is what makes bread light and fluffy when it's baked. Some breads need more kneading than others, and some breads, like focaccia, don't need to be kneaded at all!

### Here's how you do it:

1. Make sure you're working on a smooth surface, like the countertop. Some recipes tell you to flour the surface, and some don't like extra flour at all! Be sure to follow the flouring instructions in each recipe.

2. Place the dough ball in the middle of the counter.

3. Place 1 of your HANDS on top of the other, with both palms facing down. Press down onto the dough with your HANDS.

4. Using the heel of your palms, push the dough ball along the countertop away from you.

5. Next, using your HANDS, fold the dough in half, like you would fold a letter, while pulling it back toward you.

6. Do it all over again! Keep repeating steps 3–5 until the dough ball is smooth and kinda shiny!

Isn't kneading so much fun!?

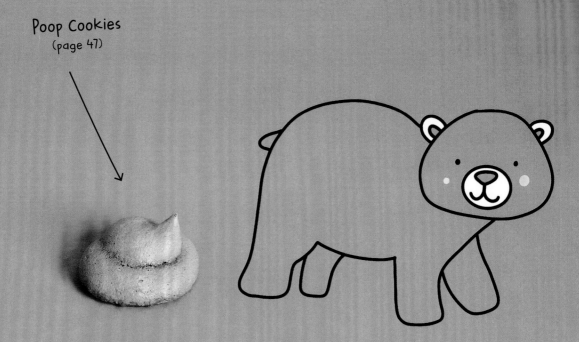

Poop Cookies
(page 47)

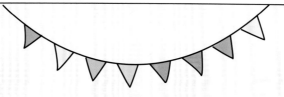

# Nifty Sifter!

Even though it's an extra thing to do, sifting is an important step for certain ingredients in some recipes. Fine powdered ingredients like flour, cocoa and powdered sugar can get lumpy when they sit around in their containers for too long. Sifting takes these lumps away and lets you create smooth, well-blended batters and doughs (like with the cocoa powder and powdered sugar in our Poop Cookies, page 47). If an ingredient needs to be sifted, it will say so in the recipe, and please be sure to sift it before continuing to bake!

## Here's how you do it:

1. Take a large bowl and place a metal mesh sifter on top of it.

2. Add the lumpy ingredient, ½ cup at a time, to the sifter.

3. Now lift the sifter up with 1 hand so it's hovering just above the bowl.

4. With your other hand, bang the sides of the sifter like you're banging a tambourine. You can sing a song if you like. Singing always makes everything fun!

5. Watch as the ingredient falls through the sifter like falling snow, leaving any lumps on top.

6. Take a spoon and smush the lumps left behind.

7. Continue sifting until all the ingredients have passed through.

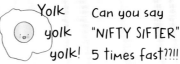

Yolk yolk yolk! Can you say "NIFTY SIFTER" 5 times fast??!!

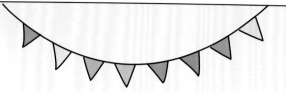

# Am I HOT or COLD?

What's the difference between a boil and a simmering boil? Who's Luke Warm anyway? Let's talk about temperature!

**Boil**: Boiling is usually done on high heat. When the ingredients in the pot form large bubbles at the bottom and rise to the top super fast, they're boiling! Boiling is noisy, and you'll see a constant cloud of steam coming from the pot.

**Simmering boil**: When the ingredients in the pot have reached a boil and then you lower the temperature but keep it hot enough so there's still a mix of big and little bubbles around the sides of the pot, you're keeping them at a simmering boil. These bubbles make a steady popping noise. There will be bursts of steam—especially when the big bubbles pop. POP!

**Lukewarm**: My temperature is somewhere between room temperature and warm. Put your hand under your armpit. That's about how warm I am. To get liquids to lukewarm temperature quickly, heat them in the microwave for 15 seconds, stir and repeat until they reach the sweet spot.

"Hi I'M Luke!"

"BRRFT!"

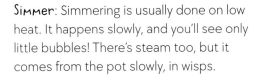

**Simmer**: Simmering is usually done on low heat. It happens slowly, and you'll see only little bubbles! There's steam too, but it comes from the pot slowly, in wisps.

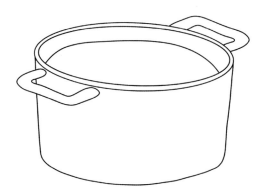

**Room temperature**: Unless you're a polar bear, at room temperature usually means the comfortable temperature of your kitchen. When a recipe calls for an ingredient to be at room temperature, simply take it out of the fridge and leave it on the counter for 1 hour before you use it.

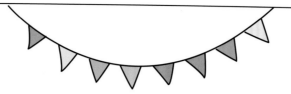

# Glazes: DIP, DUNK or DRIZZLE?

Glazes are sweeter, runnier versions of frosting. They are mostly made with powdered sugar and water and will usually harden right on top of your dessert! Here are three sweet ways to decorate donuts with glaze! And they are all gla-mazing!

## DIPPING

1. Pour your chosen glaze into a bowl. Place a cooling rack on top of a cookie sheet.

2. Hold onto the bottom of a cooled donut. Turn it upside down and dip it into the bowl of glaze. Don't let go!

3. Turn your hand back and forth a few times like you're turning an imaginary doorknob in the bowl.

4. Lift the donut out of the glaze while making one last turn with your hand. Place it glaze side up on the cooling rack to dry.

5. If you're adding a fun topping like sprinkles or toasted coconut, sprinkle it on top now before the glaze dries. Let the glaze dry completely.

6. Lick your fingers!

## DUNKING

1. Pour your chosen glaze into a bowl. Place a cooling rack on top of a cookie sheet.

2. Place your cooled donut in the bowl of glaze. Using 2 small forks, move it around the bowl gently, to coat the top, bottom and sides with the glaze.

3. Slowly lift the donut out of the glaze and place it on the cooling rack to dry.

4. If you're adding a fun topping like sprinkles or toasted coconut, sprinkle it on now before the glaze dries. Let the glaze dry completely.

5. Collect any glaze that drips onto the cookie sheet and return it to the bowl to glaze again!

6. Lick your fingers!

## DRIZZLING

1. Place a cooling rack on top of a cookie sheet. Set the cooled donuts on top of the cooling rack.

2. Fit a small piping bag with a coupler and a small round piping tip (page 34).

3. Using a big spoon, scoop your chosen glaze into the piping bag.

4. Squeeze the glaze out of the bag and over all the donuts, moving your hand back and forth to make a zigzag pattern with the glaze.

5. Collect any glaze that drips onto the cookie sheet and return it to the bag to glaze again.

6. If you're adding a fun topping like sprinkles or toasted coconut, sprinkle it on now before the glaze dries. Let the glaze dry completely.

7. Lick your fingers!

Dunked!

Drizzled!

Dipped!

# How the Cookie (Doesn't) Crumble!

Listen up! These cookies have a lot to say about baking! Follow their tips for a perfect batch!

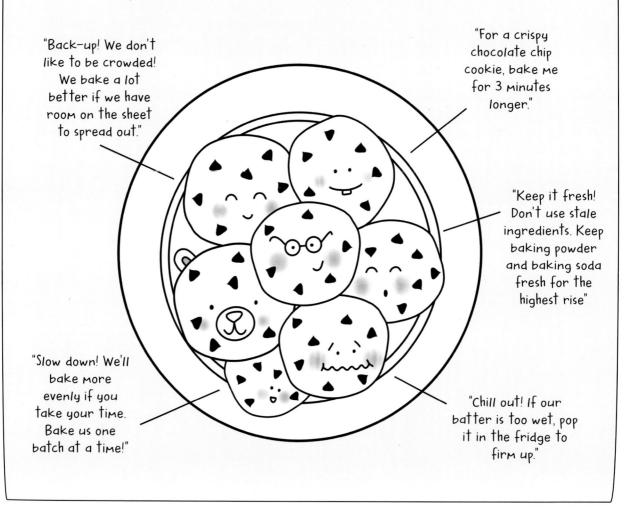

"Back-up! We don't like to be crowded! We bake a lot better if we have room on the sheet to spread out."

"For a crispy chocolate chip cookie, bake me for 3 minutes longer."

"Keep it fresh! Don't use stale ingredients. Keep baking powder and baking soda fresh for the highest rise"

"Slow down! We'll bake more evenly if you take your time. Bake us one batch at a time!"

"Chill out! If our batter is too wet, pop it in the fridge to firm up."

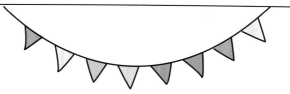

# Cupcake Decorating 1, 2, 3

Here's how to fill your cupcakes (if you'd like to) and then to make a simple swirl of frosting.

## STEP 1: FILL YOUR CUPCAKES

Add some extra flavor and fun to your cupcakes by filling them with a delicious jam and cream and mousse! Oh my! First, hollow out the center of each cupcake once it has fully cooled. You can do this three ways:

**Use an apple corer**: Get to the center of the cupcake fast by sticking an apple corer into the center of the top of the cupcake, then twist and pull it straight up.

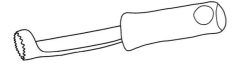

**Use a large piping tip**: These metal tips for decorating are great for making holes in cupcakes too! Simply stick the bottom (not the pointy end) of the tip into the center of the top of the cupcake. Press down and turn it. Pull it straight out.

**Use your thumb**: Yep! Your clean thumb will do the trick. Poke it into the center of the top of a cupcake. Push down on it while turning it in a circle to make a nice round hole. Thumbs up!

### Now it's time to fill!

1.  Fit a piping bag with a coupler and large round piping tip (page 34).

2.  Scoop some of your chosen frosting into the bag.

3.  Lightly squeeze the bag, squirting the filling into the hole of each cupcake until it's filled up.

## STEP 2: FROST YOUR CUPCAKES!

1.  Fit a piping bag with a coupler and large round piping tip (page 34).

2.  Scoop some of your chosen frosting into the bag.

3.  Gently squeeze a blob of the frosting, about the size of a grape, in the center of the cupcake.

4.  Now cover that blob with a hill of frosting! To do this, pipe a ring around the outside edge of the top of the cupcake. Then pipe a smaller ring inside the big one.

5.  Continue until the cupcake is covered. Sweet!

Turn to the Piping Party on page 32 for more on different piping styles.

## STEP 3: EAT YOUR CUPCAKES!

1.  Peel off the cupcake wrapper.

2.  Open your mouth (drooling is ok and to be expected).

3.  Raise the cupcake to your open mouth.

4.  Gobble the cupcake up!

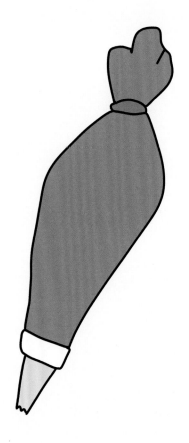

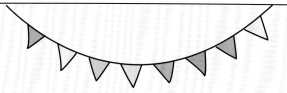

# Cake Decorating 1, 2, 3

Frosting cakes is a lot of fun! It also takes a lot of practice! In this section you'll find some useful tips and tricks to help you get started. Remember, it takes a lot of patience, so go slow and don't be upset if the first few tries come out wonky. The most important thing is to have fun. It's just dessert, after all!

## STEP 1: FILL YOUR CAKE!

Thinking about filling the middle of your cake with one of our luscious fillings? What a great idea! When you add a filling to your cake, you create an extra boost of flavor and texture in every bite.

Before filling, you must first make a dam. This is a wall of frosting that stops the filling from leaking out the sides!

## Here's how you do it:

1. Fit a large piping bag with a coupler and a large piping tip.

2. Scoop some of the frosting you plan to frost the cake with into the piping bag.

3. Gently squeeze a ring of frosting around the edge of the top of 1 of the cake layers. This is the dam!

4. Now scoop the desired filling into the center of the cake and smooth it out to the edges of the dam. See how that ring of frosting is keeping the filling in? Awesome!

5. Carefully place the next cake layer on top.

## STEP 2: COAT YOUR CAKE!

A crumb coat is a thin layer of frosting that keeps the cake crumbs glued down to your cake. Crumb coats are great because they seal in the cake's moisture and give you a nice smooth surface to frost on. Whether you're making a fancy pattern with a piping tip or simply slathering the cake in head-to-toe frosting, it's always a good idea to start with a crumb coat.

### Here's how you do it:

1. Using an offset spatula (page 198), scoop some of the frosting out of the bowl and plop it on the top of the cake. Keep doing this until there's enough frosting to cover the top surface of the cake.

2. Place the offset spatula in the center of the cake and move it back and forth like a windshield wiper to smooth and spread out the frosting into a thin layer. Extra frosting will start to fall over the sides. That's ok!

3. After you've covered the top of the cake with a thin layer of frosting, scoop, slap and smear the frosting that fell off onto the sides of the cake.

4. Hold the offset spatula straight up and down, with the handle pointing up and the blade tilted slightly. Move it around the sides of the cake, lightly smoothing out the frosting with the blade. It only needs a super-thin layer of frosting. You'll still be able to see the cake peeking through when you're done.

5. Chill the cake in the fridge or freezer for about 30 minutes to allow the crumb coat to harden before you add the second layer of frosting.

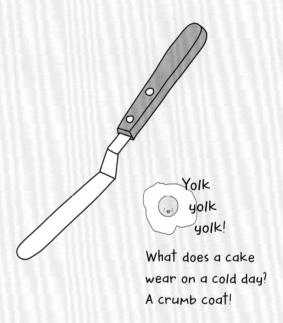

Yolk yolk yolk!

What does a cake wear on a cold day? A crumb coat!

## STEP 3: FROST YOUR CAKE!

Hooray! Now you are ready to add the final layer of frosting or, as we like to say, the last-layer-before-we-can-eat-our-cake frosting! You've done a great job so far, so keep being patient and have fun with it!

## Here's how you do it:

1. Carefully remove your cake from the fridge or freezer. Does your crumb coat feel hard when you touch it? Super, it's ready for the last layer of frosting.

2. Just like you did with the crumb coat, start by frosting the top of the cake. Using an offset spatula, scoop up some frosting from the bowl and plop it on top of the cake. Repeat until you have a nice blob of frosting on top.

3. Place the offset spatula in the center of the blob and move it back and forth like a windshield wiper. The frosting will spread out across the top of the cake. Continue doing this until you can't see the crumb coat through the frosting and the frosting is smooth and even.

4. Now on to the sides! Using the offset spatula, scoop up some of the frosting and smear it on the sides of the cake. Hold the offset spatula straight up and down, with the handle pointing up and the blade tilted slightly. Move it around the cake, lightly smoothing out the frosting with the blade. Grab more frosting when you need it.

Now you're ready to decorate! Turn to Wonderpark (page 83) for some great topping ideas. Have fun and use your imagination!

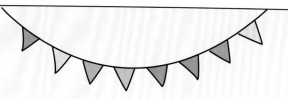

# The Piping Party!

Welcome to our piping party! You're our special guests. Here you'll learn about filling piping bags and about piping tips to help make your dessert decorating a blast! The piping tips are already here, and they want to show what kind of shapes they make when you squeeze frosting through them. May we introduce you?

Hello there! I'm Star. I love making stars and seashells.

Howdy. I'm Round. I'm great at making dots and lines!

Ciao. I'm Flower. I'm excellent at making flowers.

Bonjour, hello. I'm Leaf! Leaves are my thing, eh?!

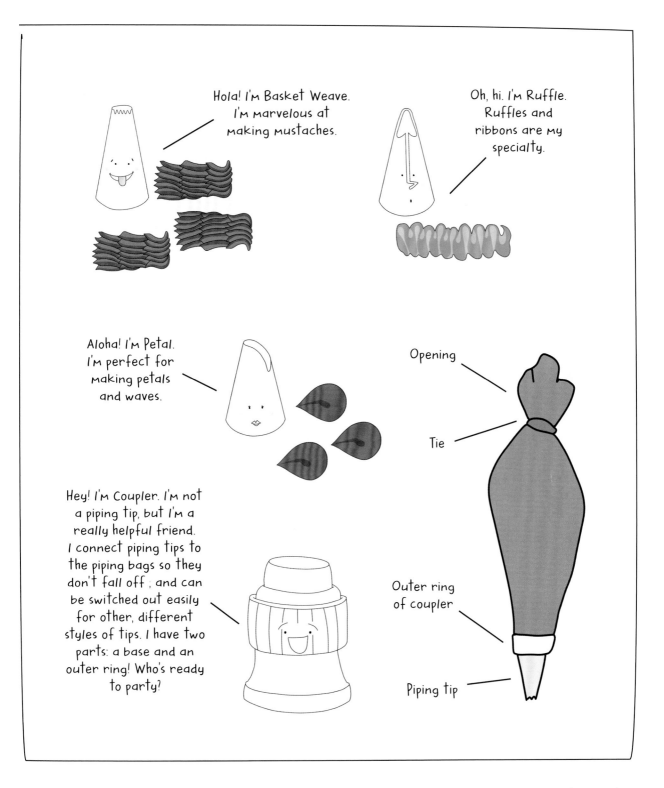

## PIPING BAGS!

Piping bags are super-handy tools when working with runny batters, filling desserts and frosting baked goods, but they can sometimes be tricky to use. As always, the more you practice with them, the easier it will get.

## Try filling them this way:

1. Start by choosing a piping tip. Piping tips and couplers come in different sizes. Make sure the tip matches the size of the coupler. You can check this by sticking the ring of the coupler over the tip. It should go on like a ring would on your finger, nice and snug. Does it fit? Super! Set this tip to the side.

2. Open the piping bag and place the base of the coupler inside the bag so the smaller, pointy end is pointing down towards the narrow end of the piping bag.

3. Pull the coupler back a little and, using scissors, snip the end of the bag to make a small hole. Slide the coupler back towards this hole. Does the top of the coupler stick out? Yes? Super! If it doesn't, snip a teeny-tiny bit more. Throw away your clippings. You don't want those in your baking!

4. Now you're ready to attach the piping tip. Stick the chosen tip on the end of the coupler's base so the pointy end is pointing out. Place the outer ring of the coupler over the piping tip. Now twist the outer ring along the coupler's base so it attaches.

5. Now you're ready to fill the bag! Look around your kitchen for a tall and tubular container. A water glass or a small vase works great. Totally tubular!

6. Stick the empty piping bag in the container, tip first. Fold the opening of the bag over the rim of the container so at least 2 inches of bag hang over the sides.

7. Using a big spoon, scoop the batter, filling or frosting into the bag and fill it up. Isn't it neat how the container is doing a great job of holding up all the stuff?!

8. Roll the bag up off the sides of the container and, using both hands, twist the bag closed.

9. Fasten the bag so nothing leaks out the opening at the top. A handy kitchen clip or elastic band will do this job! Simply clip or tie it to the twist you just made.

10. Now you're ready to pipe! Hold the piping bag with both hands, 1 at the top of the bag near the tie and the other at the bottom near the tip.

11. Gently squeeze your top hand. This will push the batter, filling or frosting down and out of the piping tip. Use your bottom hand to guide the tip to where you want it to go.

## Pipe-pipe hooray!

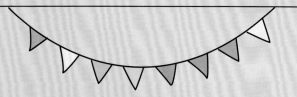

# Coloring Box

Did you know that your eye can see up to 10 million different colors? Isn't that wonderful? Think about it: that's 10 million different colors of frostings to make! Here's some great colors to get you started!

First, make a batch of your chosen frosting (the recipes to choose from are on pages 102–115). At the end of the recipe, add the food coloring. Using an electric mixer, BEAT until the color is mixed in. Here's a list of how many drops of coloring to use to get the color you want:

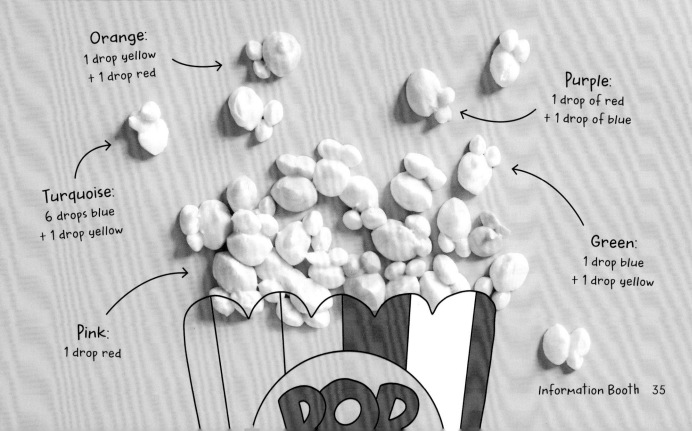

**Orange:**
1 drop yellow
+ 1 drop red

**Purple:**
1 drop of red
+ 1 drop of blue

**Turquoise:**
6 drops blue
+ 1 drop yellow

**Green:**
1 drop blue
+ 1 drop yellow

**Pink:**
1 drop red

# Chapter 1

# COOKIELAND

Take a spin on our cookie carousel! In this section, you'll find eight great cookie recipes. Whether you choose to bake our classic chocolate chip cookie or our wacky wonderland cookie, your taste buds are in for a ride! And don't just stop here. Sandwich one of our delicious frostings (page 102) or fillings (page 84) between two cookies to make the ultimate triple-decker treat! If you're looking for some extra tips on a perfect cookie-bake, get the dish on page 26. Weeeeeee!

Slam Dunk
Vanilla Milk
(page 141)

# 7th Street Chocolate Chip Cookies

## Makes 16 cookies

Growing up, we lived on 7th Street, and when our mom made these chewy chocolate chip cookies the whole street would smell like sugar. Kids would come from all over hoping to get one. Ooey-gooey when still warm from the oven, these cookies are irresistible and easy to make!

 Get Ready...

## TOOLS

- ☐ Measuring cups and spoons
- ☐ Medium saucepan
- ☐ Oven mitts
- ☐ Large bowl
- ☐ Whisk
- ☐ Small bowl
- ☐ Mixing spoon
- ☐ 2 cookie sheets
- ☐ Parchment paper or silicone baking mats
- ☐ Cooling racks

## INGREDIENTS

| ½ cup | salted butter |
|---|---|
| ¼ cup | white sugar |
| ½ cup | light brown sugar |
| 1 teaspoon | vanilla extract |
| 1 | large egg |
| 1¼ cups | all-purpose flour |
| ½ teaspoon | baking soda |
| ½ teaspoon | table salt |
| ½ cup | semisweet chocolate chips |

### There's more to explore!

Go to the **Information Booth** on page 7 to discover more about how to line your cookie sheets.

# . . . BAKE!

 1. FIND YOUR PERSON To the saucepan, add the butter. Place the saucepan on your stove. Turn the stove to low heat and gently melt the butter. Using the oven mitts, carefully remove the saucepan from the heat. Let the butter cool for 5 minutes.

 2. To the large bowl, add the white sugar, light brown sugar, cooled melted butter and vanilla extract. Using the whisk, WHISK until everything is combined. Add the egg and WHISK for 1 minute more. Set this bowl to the side.

 3. To the small bowl, add the flour, baking soda and salt. WHISK until everything is combined.

 4. Add the flour mixture to the bowl with the sugar mixture. Using the mixing spoon, MIX until the ingredients clump together and you can no longer see the flour mixture. Add the chocolate chips and MIX again.

5. Pop the bowl of cookie dough in your fridge to firm up for 15 minutes.

6. Preheat your oven to 375°F. Line the 2 cookie sheets with parchment paper or silicone baking mats.

 7. Using your HANDS, break off a piece of the cookie dough and roll it into a ball, about the size of a Ping-Pong ball. Place it on 1 of the prepared cookie sheets. Repeat until you have 8 evenly spaced cookie dough balls on each sheet.

 8. FIND YOUR PERSON Bake the cookies, 1 cookie sheet at a time, until golden brown, about 8–10 minutes.

 9. FIND YOUR PERSON Using the oven mitts, carefully remove the cookie sheets from the oven and place them on the cooling racks. Let the cookies cool completely on the cookie sheets.

**Save for later?** Store the cookies in an airtight container for up to 5 days.

 **Continue your baking adventure** in **Wonderpark** at the **Milks** (page 140)! There you can try dunking a cookie in a cold glass of flavored milk! Our favorite flavor match for these is *Slam Dunk Vanilla Milk* (page 141).

# Wonderland Cookies

These cookies are like a theme park! Filled with crunchy pretzels and chewy caramel, they're so fun! Your taste buds are sure to have a blast. Weeeeeee!

Makes 12 BIG cookies

 Get Ready...

## TOOLS

- ☐ Measuring cups and spoons
- ☐ Scissors
- ☐ Medium saucepan
- ☐ Mixing spoon
- ☐ Oven mitts
- ☐ Small bowl
- ☐ Whisk
- ☐ Large bowl
- ☐ Spatula
- ☐ Electric mixer
- ☐ 2 cookie sheets
- ☐ Parchment paper or silicone baking mats
- ☐ Cooling racks

**There's more to explore!**
Go to the **Information Booth** on page 7 to discover more about how to line your cookie sheets.

## INGREDIENTS

| | |
|---|---|
| ½ cup | salted butter |
| 1¼ cups | all-purpose flour |
| 1¼ teaspoons | baking powder |
| ¼ teaspoon | sea salt |
| ¼ cup | white sugar |
| ¾ cup | light brown sugar |
| 1 | large egg |
| ¾ cup | pretzels, some crushed into bits |
| ¼ cup | semisweet chocolate chips |
| ¼ cup | caramel candies, each cut into 4 pieces with scissors |
| ¼ cup | mini marshmallows, each cut into 4 pieces with scissors |
| ½ cup | colorful hard-shell chocolate candies |

# . . . BAKE!

1. FIND YOUR PERSON Let's make brown butter! To the saucepan, add the butter. Place the saucepan on your stove. Turn the stove to medium heat and gently melt the butter. Once the butter has melted, it will begin to foam. Using the mixing spoon, MIX it gently. Continue to cook the butter until it turns a caramel color and you see little flecks of brown. Watch it carefully. You don't want it to burn! Using the oven mitts, carefully remove the saucepan from the heat. Yay! You've just made brown butter. Let the brown butter cool for 10 minutes.

2. To the small bowl, add the flour, baking powder and salt. Using the whisk, WHISK until everything is combined. Set this bowl to the side.

3. To the large bowl, add the white sugar, light brown sugar and the cooled brown butter. Using the spatula, SCRAPE down the sides and bottom of the saucepan, adding every last drop to the bowl.

4. Using the electric mixer, BEAT on medium speed until the sugar and butter are combined, about 1 minute. Add the egg and BEAT on medium speed until everything is combined.

5. Add the flour mixture to the bowl with the sugar mixture. Using the mixing spoon, MIX until the ingredients clump together and you can no longer see the flour mixture. Add the pretzels, chocolate chips, caramels, mini marshmallows and ¼ cup of the hard-shell chocolate candies. MIX until everything is mixed in.

6. Pop the bowl of cookie dough in the fridge to firm up for 15 minutes.

7. Preheat your oven to 350°F. Line the 2 cookie sheets with the parchment paper or silicone baking mats.

8. Using your HANDS, break off a piece of the cookie dough and roll it into a ball, a bit bigger than a Ping-Pong ball. Place it on 1 of the prepared cookie sheets. Repeat until you have 6 evenly spaced cookie dough balls on each sheet.

9. Press 2–3 of the remaining chocolate candies into the top of each cookie. So wonderful!

10. FIND YOUR PERSON Bake the cookies, 1 cookie sheet at a time, until golden brown, about 8–10 minutes.

11. FIND YOUR PERSON Using the oven mitts, carefully remove the cookie sheets from the oven and place them on the cooling racks. Let the cookies cool completely on the cookie sheets.

**Save for later?** Store the cookies in an airtight container for up to 5 days.

Continue your baking adventure in **Wonderpark** at the **Milks** (page 140)! There you can try dunking a cookie in a cold glass of flavored milk! Our favorite flavor match is **Moo-vellous Strawberry Milk** (page 143).

Jam Out Berry Jam
(page 96)

# L M N O ... Peanut Butter Cookies

## Makes 16 cookies

The letter "P" stands for peanut butter! These cookies are positively perfect! Pretty and pleasing to the palate. Great for parties and picnics. We could eat them by the pant-load!

 Get Ready...

## TOOLS

- ☐ Measuring cups and spoons
- ☐ Medium saucepan
- ☐ Oven mitts
- ☐ 2 small bowls
- ☐ Whisk
- ☐ Large bowl
- ☐ Electric mixer
- ☐ Mixing spoon
- ☐ 2 cookie sheets
- ☐ Parchment paper or silicone baking mats
- ☐ Fork
- ☐ Cooling racks

## INGREDIENTS

| ½ cup | salted butter |
|---|---|
| 1¼ cups | all-purpose flour |
| ¾ teaspoon | baking soda |
| ¼ teaspoon | table salt |
| ½ cup | peanut butter, smooth or crunchy—you pick! |
| ½ cup | white sugar + ¼ cup for rolling cookies in later |
| ½ cup | light brown sugar |
| 1 | large egg |
| ½ teaspoon | vanilla extract |

### There's more to explore!

Go to the **Information Booth** on page 7 to discover more about how to line your cookie sheets.

# . . . BAKE!

1. **FIND YOUR PERSON** To the saucepan, add the butter. Place the saucepan on your stove. Turn the stove to low heat and gently melt the butter. Using the oven mitts, carefully remove the saucepan from the heat. Let the butter cool for 5 minutes.

2. To 1 of the small bowls, add the flour, baking soda and salt. Using the whisk, WHISK until everything is combined. Set this bowl to the side.

3. To the large bowl, add the cooled melted butter, peanut butter, the ½ cup of white sugar, the light brown sugar, egg and vanilla extract. Using the electric mixer, BEAT on medium-high speed until everything is combined.

4. Add the flour mixture to the bowl with the sugar mixture. Using the mixing spoon, MIX until the ingredients clump together and you can no longer see the flour mixture.

5. Pop the bowl of cookie dough in the fridge to firm up for 15 minutes.

6. Preheat your oven to 375°F. Line the 2 cookie sheets with the parchment paper or silicone baking mats. Set the cookie sheets to the side.

7. To the other small bowl, add the remaining ¼ cup of white sugar. Using your HANDS, break off a piece of the cookie dough and roll it into a ball, about the size of a Ping-Pong ball. Roll the cookie ball around in the sugar until it's sparkly on all sides. Now place it on 1 of the cookie sheets. Repeat until you have 8 evenly spaced cookie dough balls on each sheet.

8. Using the fork, press down gently on the top of each cookie twice, making a cool tic-tac-toe pattern.

9. **FIND YOUR PERSON** Bake the cookies, 1 cookie sheet at a time, until golden brown, about 8–10 minutes.

10. **FIND YOUR PERSON** Using the oven mitts, carefully remove the cookie sheets from the oven and place them on the cooling racks. Let the cookies cool completely on the cookie sheets.

**Save for later?** Store the cookies in an airtight container for up to 5 days.

Continue your baking adventure in **Wonderpark** at the **Fillings** (page 84)! There you can turn these cookies into jammy cookie sandwiches! Our favorite flavor match is **Jam Out Berry Jam!** (page 96). PB&J perfection!

Yolk yolk yolk!

How do you get a squirrel to be your friend? Act like a nut!

# Poop Cookies (GF)

## Makes lots and lots of poop cookies, depending on the size of your poop! Hee-hee!

We couldn't resist including these cheeky chocolate meringue cookies in this book.
We maybe could have called them something else . . . Butt where's the fun in that? This recipe
needs a little extra mixing muscle. A stand mixer is A MUST!

 Get Ready...

## TOOLS

- ☐ Measuring cups and spoons
- ☐ 2 cookie sheets
- ☐ Parchment paper or silicone baking mats
- ☐ 3 small bowls
- ☐ Whisk
- ☐ Large bowl
- ☐ Stand mixer with whisk attachment
- ☐ Spatula
- ☐ Big spoon
- ☐ Large piping bag
- ☐ Coupler and large round piping tip
- ☐ Oven mitts
- ☐ Cooling racks

## INGREDIENTS

| 3 tablespoons | cocoa powder |
|---|---|
| ¼ cup | powdered sugar |
| ½ cup | white sugar |
| ¼ teaspoon | cream of tartar |
| 4 | large egg whites |

### There's more to explore!
Go to the **Information Booth** on page 7 to discover more about separating eggs, piping, whipping peaks and how to line your cookie sheets.

# . . . BAKE!

1. Preheat your oven to 200°F. Line the 2 cookie sheets with parchment paper or silicone baking mats.

 2. To 1 small bowl, add the cocoa powder and powdered sugar. Using the whisk, WHISK until the mixture is lump-free. Set this bowl to the side.

 3. To the other small bowl, add the white sugar and cream of tartar. WHISK until everything is combined. Set this bowl to the side as well.

 4. FIND YOUR PERSON To the bowl of your stand mixer, add the egg whites. Beat the egg whites on medium-high speed until they're foamy, about 2 minutes. You should see lots of little bubbles! Add 1 tablespoon of the white sugar mixture to the bowl with the egg whites. Beat on low speed until everything is combined. Repeat until all the white sugar is added. Crank up the speed to high and continue to beat until stiff peaks form, 3–4 minutes.

5. Take the bowl off the stand mixer and add ¼ cup of the cocoa mixture to the bowl. Using the spatula, slowly and carefully FOLD it into the batter. Repeat until all the cocoa mixture is added and blended.

6. Using the big spoon, scoop the cookie batter into the piping bag with the coupler and large round piping tip attached.

7. Pipe the cookies onto the prepared cookie sheets. To do this, press the piping tip directly on the parchment paper. Squeeze the piping bag gently at the same time as you lift it up off the parchment paper. This will give you a nice poop shape, LOL. This cookie doesn't spread when baked, so you can fill up the cookie sheets with lots and lots of poop!

 8. FIND YOUR PERSON Bake the cookies, both sheets at the same time, for 1 hour. After 1 hour has passed, turn your oven off but leave the cookies inside your oven for another 90 minutes to cool and dry.

. . .

 9. FIND YOUR PERSON Using the oven mitts, remove the cookie sheets from the oven and place them on the cooling racks. Let the cookies dry for another 30 minutes.

Save for later? Store the cookies in an airtight container for up to 5 days.

Continue your baking adventure in **Wonderpark** at the **Milks** (page 140)! There you can try making a sweet drink to go with these cookies! Our favorite flavor matches are **Hot Cocoa** (page 148) and **Polar Bear Hot Chocolate** (page 150).

Hot Cocoa
(page 148)

Polar Bear
Hot Chocolate
(page 150)

Vanilla
Ice Scream
(page 100)

# Gingerbread Molasses Cookies

### Makes 24 cookies

Spicy and sweet with the perfect chew, these cookies are terrific but slooooooooow like molasses to make. Give yourself extra time when you're making these tasty treats, the batter needs to chill in the fridge for one hour..

## Get Ready...

## TOOLS

- ☐ Measuring cups and spoons
- ☐ Large bowl
- ☐ Electric mixer
- ☐ Medium bowl
- ☐ Mixing spoon
- ☐ Plastic wrap
- ☐ 3 cookie sheets
- ☐ Parchment paper or silicone baking mats
- ☐ Small bowl
- ☐ Oven mitts
- ☐ Cooling racks

## INGREDIENTS

| | |
|---|---|
| 1 cup | white sugar + ¼ cup for rolling cookies in later |
| ¾ cup | salted butter, at room temperature |
| ¼ cup | fancy molasses |
| 1 | large egg |
| 2¼ cups | all-purpose flour |
| 1½ teaspoons | baking soda |
| ¼ teaspoon | table salt |
| 1 teaspoon | ground cinnamon |
| ½ teaspoon | ground cloves |
| ½ teaspoon | ground ginger |
| ¼ teaspoon | ground nutmeg |

**There's more to explore!**

Go to the **Information Booth** on page 7 to discover more about room temperature and how to line your cookie sheets.

# . . . BAKE!

1. To the large bowl, add 1 cup of the white sugar, the butter, fancy molasses and egg. Using your electric mixer, BEAT on medium speed until everything is combined.

2. To the medium bowl, add the flour, baking soda, salt, ground cinnamon, ground cloves, ground ginger and ground nutmeg. Using the mixing spoon, MIX until everything is combined.

3. Add the flour mixture to the bowl with the sugar mixture. MIX until the ingredients clump together and you can no longer see the flour mixture.

4. Scoop the dough out onto a sheet of plastic wrap. Wrap it up like a burrito. Pop the dough in the fridge to firm up for 1 hour.

   . . .

5. Preheat your oven to 350°F. Line the 3 cookie sheets with the parchment paper or silicone baking mats.

6. To the small bowl, add the remaining ¼ cup of white sugar. Using your HANDS, break off a piece of the cookie dough and roll it into a ball, about the size of a Ping-Pong ball. Roll the cookie ball around in the sugar until it's sparkly on all sides. Now place it on 1 of the cookie sheets. Repeat until you have 8 evenly spaced cookie dough balls on each cookie sheet.

7. FIND YOUR PERSON Bake the cookies, 1 sheet at a time, until the tops of the cookies have cracked, about 8–10 minutes.

8. FIND YOUR PERSON Using the oven mitts, carefully remove the cookie sheets from the oven and place them on the cooling racks. Let the cookies cool completely on the cookie sheets.

   **Save for later?** Store the cookies in an airtight container for up to 5 days.

Continue your baking adventure in **Wonderpark** at the **Fillings** (page 84)! There you can try turning these cookies into ice cream sandwiches! Our favorite filling is **Vanilla Ice Scream** (page 100)!

# Goldilocks's Oatmeal Cookies

## Makes 16 cookies

These cookies aren't too sweet or too soft but JUST RIGHT! If you want, you can turn them into a spicy fall treat by adding raisins and ground cinnamon.

 Get Ready...

## TOOLS

- ☐ Measuring cups and spoons
- ☐ Medium saucepan
- ☐ Oven mitts
- ☐ Small bowl
- ☐ Whisk
- ☐ Large bowl
- ☐ Mixing spoon
- ☐ 2 cookie sheets
- ☐ Parchment paper or silicone baking mats
- ☐ Big spoon
- ☐ Cooling racks

## INGREDIENTS

| | |
|---|---|
| ½ cup | salted butter |
| ¾ cup | all-purpose flour |
| ½ teaspoon | baking soda |
| 1½ cups | quick-cooking oats |
| ⅛ teaspoon | ground cinnamon, optional |
| ½ cup | white sugar |
| ½ cup | light brown sugar |
| 1 | large egg |
| ½ teaspoon | vanilla extract |
| ½ cup | raisins, optional |

**There's more to explore!**

Go to the **Information Booth** on page 7 to discover more about how to line your cookie sheets.

# . . . BAKE!

 1. FIND YOUR PERSON To the saucepan, add the butter. Place the saucepan on your stove. Turn the stove to low heat and gently melt the butter. Using the oven mitts, carefully remove the saucepan from the heat. Let the butter cool for 5 minutes.

 2. To the small bowl, add the flour, baking soda, quick-cooking oats and ground cinnamon, if using. Using the whisk, WHISK until everything is combined. Set this bowl to the side.

 3. To the large bowl, add the cooled melted butter, white sugar, light brown sugar, egg and vanilla extract. WHISK until everything is combined.

 4. Add the flour mixture to the bowl with the sugar mixture. Using the mixing spoon, MIX until everything is combined. MIX in the raisins, if using.

5. Pop the bowl of cookie dough into the fridge to firm up for 15 minutes.

6. Preheat your oven to 375°F. Line the 2 cookie sheets with the parchment paper or silicone baking mats.

7. Using the big spoon, scoop a spoonful of cookie dough onto 1 of the prepared cookie sheets. Repeat until you have 8 evenly spaced cookie dough blobs on each sheet.

 8. FIND YOUR PERSON Bake the cookies, 1 cookie sheet at a time, until golden brown, about 8–10 minutes.

 9. FIND YOUR PERSON Using the oven mitts, carefully remove the cookie sheets from the oven and place them on the cooling racks. Let the cookies cool on the cookie sheets until they aren't too hot or too cold but just right.

**Save for later?** Store the cookies in an airtight container for up to 5 days.

Continue your baking adventure in **Wonderpark** at the **Frostings** (page 102)! There you can turn these cookies into double-decker treats! Our favorite flavor matches are **Strawberry Patch Frosting** (page 114), **Buttercream Bomb** (page 107) and **Chocolate Moose** (page 87)!

Strawberry Patch
Frosting
(page 114)

Buttercream
Bomb
(page 107)

Chocolate Moose
(page 87)

# Chocolate Fudge Cookies

## Makes 24 cookies

Dark chocolate + sea salt = a fantastic fudgy cookie with a whole lot of flavor!

 Get Ready...

## TOOLS

- ☐ Measuring cups and spoons
- ☐ Small bowl
- ☐ Whisk
- ☐ Large bowl
- ☐ Electric mixer
- ☐ Mixing spoon
- ☐ 3 cookie sheets
- ☐ Parchment paper or silicone baking mats
- ☐ Big spoon
- ☐ Oven mitts
- ☐ Cooling racks

## INGREDIENTS

| | |
|---|---|
| 1¼ cups | all-purpose flour |
| ⅓ cup | cocoa powder |
| 1 teaspoon | baking soda |
| ¾ cup | salted butter, at room temperature |
| 1 cup | white sugar |
| 1 | large egg |
| 1 teaspoon | vanilla extract |
| 1 cup | dark chocolate chips or chunks |
| ⅛ teaspoon | flaky sea salt |

### There's more to explore!

Go to the **Information Booth** on page 7 to discover more about room temperature and how to line your cookie sheets.

# . . . BAKE!

 1. To the small bowl, add the flour, cocoa powder and baking soda. Using the whisk, WHISK until everything is combined. Set this bowl to the side.

 2. To the large bowl, add the butter and white sugar. Using the electric mixer, BEAT until they're fluffy, about 2 minutes. Add the egg and vanilla extract. BEAT for 30 seconds more.

 3. Add the flour mixture to the bowl with the sugar mixture. Using the mixing spoon, MIX until the ingredients clump together and you can no longer see the flour mixture. MIX in ¾ cup of the chocolate chips or chunks.

4. Pop the bowl of cookie dough in the fridge to firm up for 15 minutes.

5. Preheat your oven to 350°F. Line the 3 cookie sheets with the parchment paper or silicone baking mats.

6. Using the big spoon, scoop a spoonful of cookie dough onto 1 of the cookie sheets. Repeat until you have 8 evenly spaced cookie dough blobs on each sheet.

7. Press the remaining chocolate chips or chunks into the top of each cookie. Sprinkle the tops with the flaky sea salt.

 8. FIND YOUR PERSON Bake the cookies, 1 cookie sheet at a time, until the tops of the cookies have cracked, about 8–10 minutes.

 9. FIND YOUR PERSON Using the oven mitts, carefully remove the cookie sheets from the oven and place them on the cooling racks. Let the cookies cool completely on the cookie sheets.

Save for later? Store the cookies in an airtight container for up to 5 days.

Continue your baking adventure in **Wonderpark** at the **Fillings** (page 84)! There you can try turning these cookies into ice cream sandwiches! Our favorite flavor is **Vanilla Ice Scream** (page 100)!

FUN FACT:  Did you know that no two tongues are alike?! A human tongue is as unique as a fingerprint! Our tongues have between 2,000 and 4,000 taste buds!

# Sugar Sugar Sugar Cookies

### Makes lots and lots of cookies, depending on which cookie cutter you use!

These sugar cookies are made with not one but three types of sugar! This unique blend of sugar gives them their sweet, buttery, melt-in-your-mouth taste and texture, multiplied by three! Rolling out cookie dough takes practice, so be patient when working with this dough. Here are some super tips to help you get started:

**Super Tip 1**: Choose a smooth, flat surface to work on. Countertops are a great choice!

**Super Tip 2**: Work with half of the dough at a time. It's much easier to roll out small balls of dough than big ones.

**Super Tip 3**: Place the dough between 2 pieces of parchment paper when rolling. This will keep the dough from sticking to your rolling pin or the surface.

**Super Tip 4**: When you're cutting out your cookie shapes, leave about a finger-width of space between each cookie. This will make it easy to pull off the scraps.

 Get Ready...

## TOOLS

- ☐ Measuring cups and spoons
- ☐ Medium saucepan
- ☐ Oven mitts
- ☐ Large bowl
- ☐ Mixing spoon
- ☐ Parchment paper
- ☐ Rolling pin
- ☐ Cookie cutters, any shape or size you like—we used ice cream shapes!
- ☐ 2 cookie sheets
- ☐ Cooling racks

## INGREDIENTS

| 1 cup | salted butter |
|---|---|
| ¼ cup | powdered sugar |
| ¼ cup | light brown sugar |
| ¼ cup | white sugar |
| 1 teaspoon | vanilla extract |
| 1 | egg, lightly beaten |
| 2¼ cups | all-purpose flour |

 There's more to explore!
Go to the **Information Booth** on page 7 to discover more about how to line your cookie sheets.

# . . . BAKE!

 1. FIND YOUR PERSON To the saucepan, add the butter. Place the saucepan on your stove. Turn the stove to low heat and gently melt the butter. Using the oven mitts, carefully remove the saucepan from the heat. Let the butter cool for 5 minutes.

2. Preheat your oven to 350°F.

 3. To the large bowl, add the powdered sugar, light brown sugar, white sugar, cooled melted butter and vanilla extract. Using the mixing spoon, MIX until everything is combined. Add the beaten egg and MIX. Add the flour and MIX until the ingredients clump together and you can no longer see the flour mixture. Let the dough rest for 10 minutes.

4. On a smooth, flat surface, lay down a sheet of parchment paper, roughly the size of a cookie sheet. Divide the cookie dough ball in half. Place one half of the cookie dough in the center of the parchment paper. Now lay another sheet of parchment paper on top of the cookie dough.

5. Using the rolling pin, roll on top of the parchment paper to flatten out the cookie dough so it's nice and smooth and ¼-inch thick. This part takes a bit of practice, as the dough is sure to slide around. When the dough is ready, peel off the top layer of parchment paper.

 6. Press the cookie cutter of your choice firmly into the flattened dough. Remove the cookie cutter by pulling straight up! Look at that! You've just made a shape! Continue to cut shapes in the dough, making sure to leave at least a finger-width of space around each cookie. This will help in the next step.

 7. Using your HANDS, peel away the scraps of dough around your cookies. Mush the scraps back into the dough ball. Now only your cookie shapes are left on the paper.

8. Carefully lift the sheet of parchment paper with the cookies and lay it on top of 1 of the cookie sheets.

9. Get a brand-new sheet of parchment paper and repeat steps 4–8 with the remaining dough!

 10. FIND YOUR PERSON Bake the cookies, 1 cookie sheet at a time, until golden brown, about 8–10 minutes.

11. FIND YOUR PERSON Using the oven mitts, carefully remove the cookie sheets from the oven and place them on the cooling racks. Let the cookies cool completely on the cookie sheets.

**Save for later?** Store the cookies in an airtight container for up to 5 days.

Continue your baking adventure in **Wonderpark** at the **Glazes and More** (page 116). There you can make a sweet coating for these cookies! Our favorite flavor is **Her Royal Highness Icing** (page 118), which can be tinted all the colors of the rainbow, and topped with sprinkles!

Her Royal Highness Icing
(page 118)

# Chapter 2

The sky's the limit when it comes to the flavor combinations you can come up with here! In this section, you'll discover recipes for six scrumptious cupcakes, perfect for filling AND frosting AND topping! This lil' baked good can do it all! Now it's up, up and away with your imagination!

Buttercream
Bomb
(page 107)

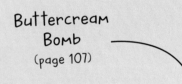

# Rainbow Cupcakes

### Makes 18 cupcakes

What would you get if a fluffy vanilla cupcake wrestled a unicorn? Our rainbow cupcakes, of course! It takes a little extra time to dye the cupcake batter six different colors, and your kitchen might be a colorful mess when you're through, but it's well worth it! We highly recommend using food coloring gel for this recipe, as the colors stay nice and bright after baking.

 Get Ready...

## TOOLS

- ☐ Measuring cups and spoons
- ☐ Sifter
- ☐ 2 muffin pans
- ☐ Cupcake liners
- ☐ Large bowl
- ☐ Whisk
- ☐ Electric mixer
- ☐ Big spoon
- ☐ 6 small bowls
- ☐ 6 small spoons
- ☐ Oven mitts
- ☐ Toothpicks
- ☐ Cooling racks

## INGREDIENTS

| | |
|---|---|
| Cooking spray, for greasing pans | |
| 1½ cups | all-purpose flour, sifted |
| ½ cup | cake and pastry flour |
| 1 cup | white sugar |
| 1 cup | light brown sugar |
| 1 teaspoon | baking powder |
| 1 teaspoon | baking soda |
| 1 teaspoon | table salt |
| ¾ cup | vegetable oil |
| 1 | large egg |
| 1 | large egg yolk |
| 1 cup | buttermilk |
| 2½ teaspoons | vanilla extract |
| ½ cup | boiling water |
| Food coloring gel in 6 colors | red, orange, yellow, green, blue and purple |

### There's more to explore!

Go to the **Information Booth** on page 7 to discover more about sifting, separating eggs, preparing your muffin pans and frosting your cupcakes.

# . . . BAKE!

1. Preheat your oven to 350°F. Take the 2 muffin pans and place cupcake liners in 18 of the cups. Spray the inside of the liners with cooking spray.

2. To the large bowl, add the all-purpose flour, cake and pastry flour, white sugar, light brown sugar, baking powder, baking soda and salt. Using the whisk, WHISK until the mixture is lump-free.

3. Slowly add the vegetable oil, egg and egg yolk, buttermilk and vanilla extract. Using the electric mixer, BEAT on low speed until everything is combined.

4. FIND YOUR PERSON Slowly and carefully add the boiling water.

5. Gently WHISK until everything is combined.

6. Using the big spoon, scoop equal amounts of the batter into each of the 6 small bowls.

7. Dip 1 small spoon into 1 of the food coloring gels, then stir the spoon around in 1 of the bowls of batter. Continue to stir until the color is mixed in. Keep that spoon in that bowl.

8. Repeat step 7 for the other bowls of batter until all the batters are dyed a different color of the rainbow! So pretty!

9. Once all the batter is dyed, scoop a spoonful of each of the colored batters, one at a time, into each cupcake liner until the cupcake liners are filled ⅔ of the way up with batter.

10. FIND YOUR PERSON Bake the cupcakes, 1 muffin pan at a time, until a toothpick stuck in the middle of a cupcake comes out clean, 15–17 minutes.

11. FIND YOUR PERSON Using the oven mitts, carefully remove the muffin pans from the oven and place them on the cooling racks. Let the cupcakes cool completely before removing them from the pans.

Save for later? Store the cupcakes in an airtight container for up to 3 days.

Continue your baking adventure in **Wonderpark** at the **Frostings** (page 102). There you can try slathering these cupcakes with a fabulous frosting! Our favorite flavor match is **Buttercream Bomb** (page 107).

How high do you fill a cupcake liner? 2/3 of the way full

The sweet spot

# Chocolate Ker-Pow Cupcakes

### Makes 18 cupcakes

We're not messing around. These chocolate cupcakes pack an awesome chocolatey punch!
Would you believe the secret ingredient to their rich chocolatey flavor is coffee?
Don't worry, there's not enough coffee in here to keep you up at night, maybe just enough
to put a little hair on your chest . . . just kidding!

 Get Ready. . .

## TOOLS

- ☐ Measuring cups and spoons
- ☐ Sifter
- ☐ 2 muffin pans
- ☐ Cupcake liners
- ☐ Large bowl
- ☐ Whisk
- ☐ Electric mixer
- ☐ Spatula
- ☐ Big spoon
- ☐ Spouted measuring cup
- ☐ Toothpicks
- ☐ Oven mitts
- ☐ Cooling racks

## INGREDIENTS

| | |
|---|---|
| Cooking spray, for greasing pans | |
| 1 cup | all-purpose flour |
| ½ cup | cake and pastry flour |
| 1½ cups | light brown sugar |
| ½ cup | cocoa powder, sifted |
| 1½ teaspoons | baking soda |
| ¾ teaspoon | baking powder |
| ¼ teaspoon | table salt |
| ½ cup | vegetable oil |
| 1 | large egg |
| 1 | large egg yolk |
| ¾ cup | buttermilk |
| ½ cup | freshly brewed coffee |
| 1 teaspoon | vanilla extract |
| ¼ cup | boiling water |

### There's more to explore!

Go to the **Information Booth** on page 7 to
discover more about sifting, separating eggs
and preparing your muffin pans.

# . . . BAKE!

1. Preheat your oven to 350°F. Take the 2 muffin pans and place cupcake liners in 18 of the cups. Spray the inside of the liners with cooking spray.

2. To the large bowl, add the all-purpose flour, cake and pastry flour, light brown sugar, cocoa powder, baking soda, baking powder and salt. Using the whisk, WHISK until the mixture is lump-free.

3. Add the vegetable oil, egg and egg yolk, buttermilk, brewed coffee and vanilla extract. Using the electric mixer, BEAT on low speed until everything is combined.

4. FIND YOUR PERSON Slowly and carefully add the boiling water.

5. Gently WHISK until everything is combined.

6. Using the spatula, SCRAPE down the sides and bottom of the bowl.

7. Using the big spoon, scoop the batter into the spouted measuring cup. Pour the batter into each cupcake liner, filling them ⅔ of the way up.

8. FIND YOUR PERSON Bake the cupcakes, 1 muffin pan at a time, until a toothpick stuck in the middle of a cupcake comes out clean, about 16–18 minutes.

9. FIND YOUR PERSON Using the oven mitts, carefully remove the muffin pans from the oven and place them on the cooling racks. Let the cupcakes cool completely before removing them from the pans.

Save for later? Store the cupcakes in an airtight container for up to 3 days.

How high do you fill a cupcake liner? 2/3 of the way full

The sweet spot

Continue your baking adventure in **Wonderpark** at the **Frostings** (page 102). There you can try frosting these cupcakes with one of our dreamy frostings. Our favorite flavor match is **Chocolate Milky Way Frosting** (page 105) topped with edible gold star sprinkles!

FUN FACT:  Chocolate and coffee are neighbors! Both beans grow on tropical plants that live just north and south of the equator. This place is called "The Bean Belt"! Have you ever *bean* there?

Chocolate Milky
Way Frosting
(page 105)

Yolk yolk yolk!

Why did the banana go to the doctor? Because it wasn't peeling well.

BING! Cherry Compote (page 94)

# Banana-nana Cupcakes Ⓥ

## Makes 18 cupcakes

Hold the banana phone! We've gone bananas for these tender and tasty vegan cupcakes!
Be sure to use very ripe bananas for the best 'nana flavor!

 Get Ready...

## TOOLS

- ☐ Measuring cups and spoons
- ☐ 2 muffin pans
- ☐ Cupcake liners
- ☐ Large bowl
- ☐ Whisk
- ☐ Electric mixer
- ☐ Spatula
- ☐ Big spoon
- ☐ Spouted measuring cup
- ☐ Toothpicks
- ☐ Oven mitts
- ☐ Cooling racks

## INGREDIENTS

| | |
|---|---|
| Cooking spray, for greasing pans | |
| 2 cups | all-purpose flour |
| ¾ cup | cake and pastry flour |
| 2 cups | white sugar |
| 1 teaspoon | baking soda |
| 1 teaspoon | table salt |
| 2 | very ripe bananas, mushed until there are hardly any lumps |
| ½ cup | vegetable oil |
| 1½ tablespoons | vanilla extract |
| ½ teaspoon | banana extract |
| 1½ cups | boiling water |

### There's more to explore!
Go to the **Information Booth** on page 7 to discover more about preparing your muffin pans.

# . . . BAKE!

1. Preheat your oven to 350°F. Take the 2 muffin pans and place cupcake liners in 18 of the cups. Spray the inside of the liners with cooking spray.

2. To the large bowl, add the all-purpose flour, cake and pastry flour, white sugar, baking soda and salt. Using the whisk, WHISK until the mixture is lump-free.

3. Add the very ripe bananas, vegetable oil and vanilla and banana extracts. Using the electric mixer, BEAT on low speed until everything is combined.

4. FIND YOUR PERSON Slowly and carefully add the boiling water to the bowl.

5. Gently WHISK until everything is combined.

6. Using the spatula, SCRAPE down the sides and bottom of the bowl.

7. Using the big spoon, scoop the batter into the spouted measuring cup. Pour the batter into each cupcake liner, filling them ⅔ of the way up.

8. FIND YOUR PERSON Bake the cupcakes, 1 muffin pan at a time, until a toothpick stuck in the middle of a cupcake comes out clean, 16–18 minutes.

9. FIND YOUR PERSON Using the oven mitts, carefully remove the muffin pans from the oven and place them on the cooling racks. Let the cupcakes cool completely before removing them from the pans.

**Save for later?** Store the cupcakes in an airtight container for up to 3 days.

How high do you fill a cupcake liner? 2/3 of the way full

The sweet spot

**Continue your baking adventure** in **Wonderpark** at the **Fillings** (page 84)! There you can try these cupcakes with a fantastic filling! Our favorite vegan flavor match is **BING! Cherry Compote** (page 94). If you'd like to frost them too, try **Marvelous Mallow Frosting** (page 109). Why? Because it's marvelous, of course!!

# Vanilla Cloud-Cakes

### Makes 18 cupcakes

Fluffy and packed with a sweet vanilla flavor, these gluten-free cupcakes are a dream!

| TOOLS |
|---|
| ☐ Measuring cups and spoons |
| ☐ 2 metal muffin pans—not silicone! |
| ☐ Cupcake liners |
| ☐ Small bowl |
| ☐ Whisk |
| ☐ Large bowl |
| ☐ Electric mixer |
| ☐ Big spoon |
| ☐ Toothpicks |
| ☐ Oven mitts |
| ☐ Cooling racks |

## INGREDIENTS

| Cooking spray, for greasing pans | |
|---|---|
| 1½ cups | gluten-free 1:1 baking flour |
| 2 teaspoons | baking powder |
| ½ cup | salted butter, at room temperature |
| ¾ cup | white sugar |
| 2 | large eggs |
| 2½ teaspoons | vanilla bean paste |
| ½ cup | whole milk |

### There's more to explore!

Go to the **Information Booth** on page 7 to discover more about room temperature and preparing your muffin pans.

# . . . BAKE!

1. Preheat your oven to 350°F. Take the 2 muffin pans and place cupcake liners in 18 of the cups. Spray the inside of the liners with cooking spray.

2. To the small bowl, add the gluten-free flour and baking powder. Using the whisk, WHISK until everything is combined. Set this bowl to the side.

3. To the large bowl, add the butter and white sugar. Using the electric mixer, BEAT on medium-high speed until they're light and fluffy. Add the eggs and vanilla bean paste. BEAT on low speed until everything is combined.

4. Now add half of the flour mixture and half of the milk. BEAT on low speed until combined. Add the rest of the flour mixture and milk and BEAT on low speed until everything is combined.

5. Using the big spoon, scoop the batter into each cupcake liner, filling them ⅔ of the way up.

6. FIND YOUR PERSON Bake the cupcakes, 1 muffin pan at a time, until a toothpick stuck in the middle of a cupcake comes out clean, 18–20 minutes.

7. FIND YOUR PERSON Using the oven mitts, carefully remove the muffin pans from the oven and place them on a cooling racks. Let the cupcakes cool completely before removing them from the pans.

**Save for later?** Store the cupcakes in an airtight container for up to 3 days.

How high do you fill a cupcake liner? 2/3 of the way full

The sweet spot

Continue your baking adventure in **Wonderpark** at the **Fillings** (page 84) and the **Frostings** (page 102)! There you can fill these treats with one of our velvety fillings—like **Princess Banana Lips** (page 98)—and then frost them with **Fluffy Cream Cheese Frosting** tinted pink (page 111)!

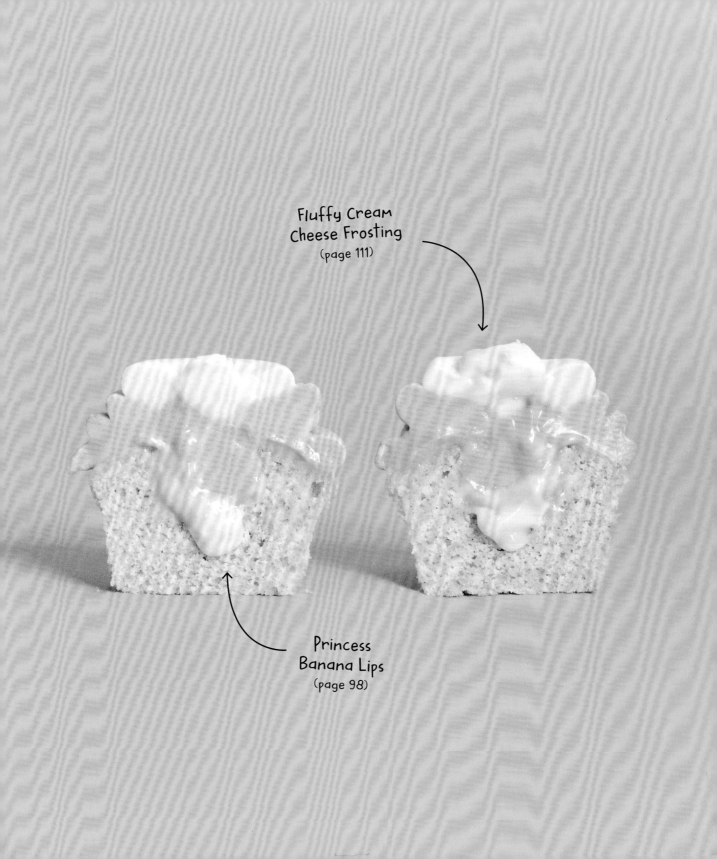

Fluffy Cream
Cheese Frosting
(page 111)

Princess
Banana Lips
(page 98)

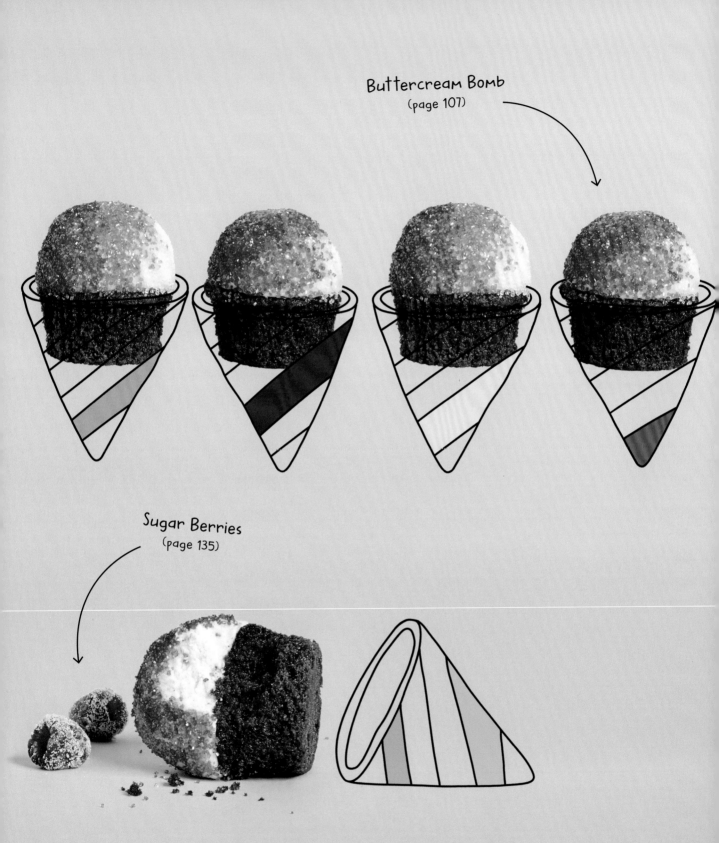

Buttercream Bomb
(page 107)

Sugar Berries
(page 135)

# Ruby Red Velvet Cupcakes

### Makes 24 cupcakes

What's chocolate and vanilla and red all over? Our Ruby Red Velvet Cupcakes! These cupcakes have a lovely chocolate and vanilla flavor and their bright red color makes them so much fun to decorate—but even more fun to eat! We'll take two scoops with sprinkles on top, please!

 Get Ready...

## TOOLS

- ☐ Measuring cups and spoons
- ☐ 2 muffin pans
- ☐ Cupcake liners
- ☐ Large bowl
- ☐ Whisk
- ☐ Electric mixer
- ☐ Spatula
- ☐ Spouted measuring cup
- ☐ Toothpicks
- ☐ Oven mitts
- ☐ Cooling racks

**There's more to explore!**
Go to the *Information Booth* on page 7 to discover more about preparing your muffin pans.

## INGREDIENTS

| | |
|---|---|
| Cooking spray, for greasing pans | |
| 1½ cups | all-purpose flour |
| ½ cup | cake and pastry flour |
| 2 cups | white sugar |
| 2 tablespoons | cocoa powder |
| 1 teaspoon | baking powder |
| 1 teaspoon | baking soda |
| 1 teaspoon | table salt |
| 2 | large eggs |
| 1 cup | buttermilk |
| ¾ cup | vegetable oil |
| 2 teaspoons | vanilla extract |
| 1 teaspoon | white vinegar |
| 1 (1 ounce/28 ml) jar | liquid red food coloring—yep, the WHOLE jar! |
| ½ cup | boiling water |

# . . . BAKE!

1. Preheat your oven to 350°F. Take the 2 muffin pans and place cupcake liners in each of the cups. Spray the inside of the liners with cooking spray.

2. To the large bowl, add the all-purpose flour, cake and pastry flour, white sugar, cocoa powder, baking powder, baking soda and salt. Using the whisk, WHISK until the mixture is lump-free.

3. Add the eggs, buttermilk, vegetable oil, vanilla extract, white vinegar and liquid red food coloring. Using the electric mixer, BEAT on low speed until everything is combined.

4. FIND YOUR PERSON Slowly and carefully add the boiling water.

5. Gently WHISK until everything is combined. The batter should be very wet.

6. Using the spatula, SCRAPE the batter into the spouted measuring cup. SCRAPE down the sides and bottom of the bowl. Pour the batter into each cupcake liner, filling them ⅔ of the way up.

7. FIND YOUR PERSON Bake the cupcakes, 1 muffin pan at a time, until a toothpick stuck in the middle of a cupcake comes out clean, about 16–18 minutes.

8. FIND YOUR PERSON Using the oven mitts, carefully remove the muffin pans from the oven and place them on the cooling racks. Let the cupcakes cool completely before removing them from the pans.

Save for later? Store the cupcakes in an airtight container for up to 3 days.

How high do you fill a cupcake liner? 2/3 of the way full

The sweet spot

Continue your baking adventure in **Wonderpark** at the **Frostings** (page 102) and **Toppings** (page 128)! There you can frost and top these cupcakes with one of our rad toppings! Our favorite flavor match is **Buttercream Bomb** (page 107) topped with **Sugar Berries** (page 135) and a whole lot of sprinkles!

# Cinnamon Hug Cupcakes

### Makes 24 cupcakes

We heart the spicy cinnamon flavor you get from these cupcakes. The layering effect takes a little bit more time to create but is totally worth the work. Every bite is like a warm hug. Now let's hug it out!

 Get Ready...

## TOOLS

- ☐ Measuring cups and spoons
- ☐ 2 small bowls
- ☐ Whisk
- ☐ 2 muffin pans
- ☐ Cupcake liners
- ☐ Large bowl
- ☐ Big spoon
- ☐ Spouted measuring cup
- ☐ Toothpicks
- ☐ Oven mitts
- ☐ Cooling racks

**There's more to explore!**
Go to the **Information Booth** on page 7 to discover more about room temperature and preparing your muffin pans.

## INGREDIENTS

### Cinnamon Swirl

| | |
|---|---|
| 1½ tablespoons | ground cinnamon |
| 2 tablespoons | light brown sugar |
| 2½ tablespoons | white sugar |

### Cupcakes

| | |
|---|---|
| Cooking spray, for greasing pans | |
| 1¼ cups | cake and pastry flour |
| 1½ teaspoons | ground cinnamon |
| 1¼ teaspoons | baking powder |
| 1 teaspoon | baking soda |
| ½ teaspoon | table salt |
| 2 | large eggs, at room temperature |
| ¾ cup | white sugar |
| ½ cup | canola oil |
| ½ cup | sour cream, at room temperature |
| 2 teaspoons | vanilla extract |
| ¼ cup | boiling water |

# . . . BAKE!

## Cinnamon Swirl

 1. To 1 small bowl, add the ground cinnamon, light brown sugar and white sugar. Using the whisk, WHISK until everything is combined. Set this bowl to the side.

## Cupcakes

1. Preheat your oven to 350°F. Take the 2 muffin pans and place cupcake liners in each of the cups. Spray the inside of the liners with cooking spray.

 2. To the other small bowl, add the cake and pastry flour, ground cinnamon, baking powder, baking soda and salt. WHISK until everything is combined. Set this bowl to the side.

 3. To the large bowl, add the eggs and white sugar. WHISK until they're frothy, about 1 minute. Add the canola oil, sour cream and vanilla extract and WHISK until everything is combined.

 4. Add the flour mixture to the eggy mixture. WHISK until everything is combined.

5. FIND YOUR PERSON Slowly and carefully add the boiling water and WHISK until the water is combined into the batter.

6. Using the big spoon, scoop the batter into the spouted measuring cup. Pour about 1 tablespoon of cupcake batter into each cupcake liner.

7. Next, sprinkle each cupcake with ¼ teaspoon of the cinnamon swirl. Continue to fill the cupcake liners, switching between the batter and the cinnamon swirl until the cupcake liners are filled ⅔ of the way up.

8. Stick a toothpick into the center of each cupcake and swirl the batter around to create a neat ripple! Sprinkle the top of each cupcake with ¼ teaspoon of cinnamon swirl.

 9. FIND YOUR PERSON Bake the cupcakes, 1 muffin pan at a time, until a toothpick stuck in the middle of a cupcake comes out clean, 12–14 minutes.

 10. FIND YOUR PERSON Using the oven mitts, carefully remove the muffin pans from the oven and place them on the cooling racks. Let the cupcakes cool completely before removing them from the pans.

**Save for later?** Store the cupcakes in an airtight container for up to 3 days.

How high do you fill a cupcake liner? 2/3 of the way full

The sweet spot

Continue your baking adventure in **Wonderpark** at the **Frostings** (page 102) and **Toppings** (page 128)! There you can pick a frosting for your cupcakes and add a fun topping to bedazzle them with! Our favorite flavor matches are **Fluffy Cream Cheese Frosting** (page 111) topped with a sprinkling of **Cinnamon Sugar** (page 139)!

Fluffy Cream
Cheese Frosting
(page 111)

Cinnamon Sugar
(page 139)

Yolk yolk yolk!

Why did the cinnamon roll? Because he saw the cherry turnover!

# Chapter 3

# WONDERPARK

Welcome to Wonderpark, the sweet center of Baking Wonderland! Here you can discover recipes to go on, in and around your baking creation. Have fun playing with flavors, there are so many combinations to try!

# FILLINGS

Fillings are fantastic, aren't they? They're like a surprise party for your mouth. Mostly because you don't know they're there until you take a bite—surprise! Enjoy your ride on the filling river!

# White Chocolate Dream  (GF)

### Make about 3 cups (photo on page 182)

On the night before baking, visions of white chocolate will dance in your head . . .
This filling is DREAMY, but it needs a little extra time to set up. In fact,
you have to make it the night before! Sleepover party? Yes, please!

 Get Ready...

| TOOLS |
|---|
| ☐ Measuring cups and spoons |
| ☐ Medium saucepan |
| ☐ Oven mitts |
| ☐ Large bowl |
| ☐ Whisk |
| ☐ Plastic wrap |
| ☐ Electric mixer |

| INGREDIENTS | |
|---|---|
| 1½ cups | whipping cream |
| 1 tablespoon | vanilla bean paste |
| ¼ teaspoon | cream of tartar |
| ½ cup | white chocolate chips |

**There's more to explore!**
Go to the **Information Booth** on page 7 to
discover more about whipping peaks.

# . . . BAKE!

 1. FIND YOUR PERSON To the saucepan, add the whipping cream and vanilla bean paste. Place the saucepan on your stove. Turn the stove to medium-high heat and bring this mixture to a simmer. Watch it carefully. It won't take long!

 2. FIND YOUR PERSON Using the oven mitts, carefully remove the saucepan from the heat. Slowly and carefully pour the mixture into the large bowl.

 3. Add the cream of tartar to the bowl. Using the whisk, WHISK until the cream of tartar disappears. Add the chocolate chips. WHISK until the chips have melted. Once they've melted, WHISK for 1 minute more.

4. Cover the bowl of cream with a sheet of plastic wrap. Carefully place the bowl in your fridge to set overnight. Go to bed (don't forget to brush your teeth)!

. . .

 5. The next day, remove the plastic wrap. Using the electric mixer, BEAT the cream mixture on high speed until stiff peaks form, about 4 minutes. Dreamy!

**Save for later?** Store the cream in an airtight container in the fridge for up to 5 days.

Continue your baking adventure in **Cakeland** (page 175)! There you can try making a tasty cake to layer with this cream. Our favorite flavor match is **Confetti Cake** (page 183)!

# Chocolate Moose  (GF)

Makes about 2 cups (photo on page 55)

This delicious and absolutely decadent chocolate filling takes only two ingredients to make. Smoosh it in between cookies, stuff it in cupcakes or eat it right out of the bowl. It's a moose-try!

 Get Ready...

## TOOLS

☐ Measuring cups and spoons
☐ Large heatproof bowl
☐ Medium saucepan
☐ Whisk
☐ Oven mitts
☐ Plastic wrap
☐ Electric mixer

## INGREDIENTS

| 1½ cups | semisweet chocolate chips |
| 1¼ cups | whipping cream |

**There's more to explore!**
Go to the *Information Booth* on page 7 to discover more about boiling points.

# . . . BAKE!

1. To the large heatproof bowl, add the chocolate chips. Set this bowl to the side.

2. FIND YOUR PERSON To the saucepan, add 1 cup of the whipping cream. Place the saucepan on the stove. Turn the stove to medium heat and bring the cream to a simmer.

3. Using the whisk, WHISK the cream the whole time it's heating. Watch it carefully. It won't take long!

4. FIND YOUR PERSON Using the oven mitts, carefully remove the saucepan from the heat. Slowly and carefully pour the hot cream into the bowl of chocolate.

3. WHISK until the chocolate chips have melted. Add the remaining ¼ cup of whipping cream and WHISK until combined.

6. Carefully place the bowl in your fridge to cool for 1 hour.

. . .

7. Using the electric mixer, BEAT the cream on medium-high speed for 3 minutes until it's light and fluffy. Ta da!

**Save for later?** Store the moose in an airtight container in the fridge for up to 1 week.

Continue your baking adventure in **Cookieland** (page 37)! Our favorite flavor match is **Goldilocks's Oatmeal Cookies** (page 53)!

# Bonjour! Pastry Cream (GF)

## Makes about 2 cups

Say "Bonjour" to smooth, silky pastry cream that comes together in a snap. The trick to this recipe is to work with two saucepans: one to warm the milk and the other to hold the ingredients. This recipe needs 4 hours to set up in the fridge, so plan ahead!

## TOOLS

- ☐ Measuring cups and spoons
- ☐ 2 medium saucepans
- ☐ Whisk
- ☐ Oven mitts
- ☐ Sifter
- ☐ Large heatproof bowl
- ☐ Spatula
- ☐ Plastic wrap

## INGREDIENTS

| | |
|---|---|
| 2 cups | whole milk |
| ¼ cup | white sugar |
| 3 tablespoons | cornstarch |
| ⅛ teaspoon | table salt |
| 4 | large egg yolks |
| 3 tablespoons | salted butter, at room temperature |
| 1 tablespoon | vanilla extract |

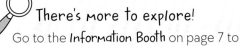

### There's more to explore!

Go to the **Information Booth** on page 7 to discover more about separating eggs and boiling points.

# . . . BAKE!

 Made on the stove, this recipe needs YOUR PERSON with you the whole time.

1. To 1 saucepan, add the milk. Place the saucepan on your stove. Turn the stove to medium heat and bring the milk to a simmer. Watch it carefully. You don't want it to boil!

 2. To the other saucepan, off the heat, add the white sugar, cornstarch, salt and egg yolks. Using the whisk, WHISK until everything is combined. The mixture should look like a thick yellow paste.

3. Using the oven mitts, carefully remove the saucepan with the hot milk from the heat. Slowly and carefully pour the hot milk into the saucepan with the sugar mixture.

 4. WHISK until everything is combined.

5. Place the saucepan with the milk and sugar mixture on your stove. Turn the stove to medium heat and bring this mixture to a boil. Using the whisk, WHISK it the whole time it's heating. Once it's boiling, reduce the heat to low and simmer until it thickens, about 2 minutes.

 6. Using your oven mitts, carefully remove the saucepan from the heat. Add the butter and vanilla extract. WHISK until the butter is completely melted.

7. Place the sifter on top of the large heatproof bowl and pour the thickened cream through the sifter. This should get rid of any unwanted lumps or bumps!

8. Lay a large sheet of plastic wrap over the bowl and press down so the plastic wrap is touching the cream. This will keep the cream nice and soft while chilling.

9. Carefully place the bowl of cream in your fridge to chill for about 4 hours.

**Save for later?** Store the cream in an airtight container in the fridge for up to 3 days.

 Continue your baking adventure in **Cakeland** (page 175)! There you can try baking some delish cakes to layer with this cream! Our favorite flavor match is **Lemony Olive Oil Cake** (page 191)!

 Yolk yolk yolk! Did you know that pastries have been around since the time of Ancient Egypt? They had a lot of mummies to make them.

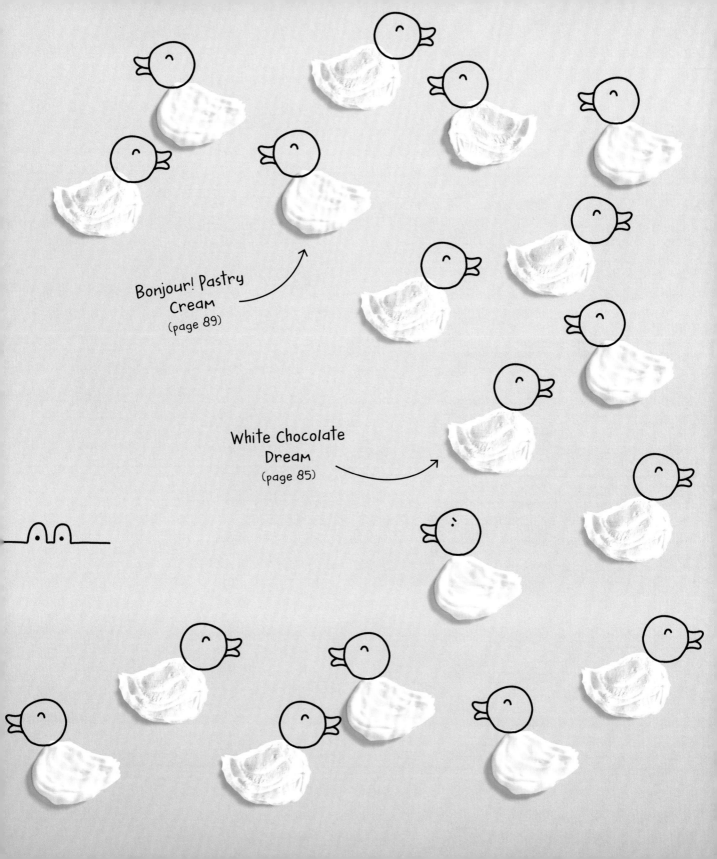

Bonjour! Pastry
Cream
(page 89)

White Chocolate
Dream
(page 85)

# Fudge! Filling (GF)

Makes about 2 cups (photo on page 181)

Chocolate fudge belongs EVERYWHERE, but especially piped into the center of a dessert! Smooth and chocolatey, this filling is fantastic.

## ☑ Get Ready...

### TOOLS

- ☐ Measuring cups and spoons
- ☐ Sifter
- ☐ Medium saucepan
- ☐ Mixing spoon
- ☐ Oven mitts
- ☐ Medium heatproof bowl
- ☐ Spatula

### INGREDIENTS

| | |
|---|---|
| ⅔ cup | whipping cream |
| ½ cup | light or dark corn syrup |
| ⅓ cup | light brown sugar |
| ¼ cup | cocoa powder, sifted |
| ⅓ cup | semisweet chocolate chips |
| ⅓ cup | dark chocolate chips |
| 2 tablespoons | salted butter |
| 2 teaspoons | vanilla extract |

**There's more to explore!**
Go to the *Information Booth* on page 7 to discover more about boiling points.

# . . . BAKE!

 Made on the stove, this recipe needs YOUR PERSON with you the whole time.

1. To the saucepan, add the whipping cream, corn syrup, light brown sugar, cocoa powder and semisweet chocolate chips. Place the saucepan on your stove. Turn the stove to medium-high heat and bring this mixture to a boil. Using the mixing spoon, MIX the whole time it's heating.

 2. Once the mixture has come to a boil, reduce the heat to low and cook at a simmering boil for 5 minutes. Keep MIX-ing!

3. Using the oven mitts, carefully remove the saucepan from the heat. Add the dark chocolate chips, butter and vanilla extract to the saucepan. MIX until the mixture is smooth.

FUN FACT: The story goes that fudge got  its name when a baker was trying to make caramel. When the recipe went wrong, they exclaimed, "Oh, fudge!"

 4. Using the oven mitts, carefully pour the fudge (it should be runny) into the medium heatproof bowl. Using the spatula, SCRAPE down the sides and bottom of the saucepan, adding every last drop to the bowl.

5. Pop the bowl of fudge in your fridge to thicken for 1 hour.

Save for later? Store the fudge in an airtight container in the fridge for up to 3 weeks. Gently reheat the fudge in the microwave or on the stove before you use it.

Continue your baking adventure in **Cakeland** (page 175)! Try layering a cake with this chocolatey goo! Our favorite flavor match is **Disappearing Chocolate Cake** (page 179)!

# BING! Cherry Compote

## Makes about 2 cups (photo on page 70)

What's better than a cherry on top? A sweet cherry filling smack-dab in the middle of a dessert! For ease, we use frozen Bing cherries in this recipe, but any variety of cherry will do. Feel free to use fresh cherries—just don't forget to remove the pits. It's the pits to bite down on one!

 ✓ Get Ready...

| TOOLS |
|---|
| ☐ Measuring cups and spoons |
| ☐ Medium saucepan |
| ☐ Mixing spoon |
| ☐ Small bowl |
| ☐ Whisk |
| ☐ Oven mitts |
| ☐ Medium heatproof bowl |
| ☐ Spatula |
| ☐ Fork |

| INGREDIENTS | |
|---|---|
| 2 cups | pitted Bing cherries, fresh or frozen |
| ¼ cup | white sugar |
| ½ tablespoon | freshly squeezed orange juice |
| ½ teaspoon | orange zest |
| 1 tablespoon | cornstarch |
| 2 tablespoons | cold water |

**There's more to explore!**
Go to the *Information Booth* on page 7 to discover more about boiling points.

# . . . BAKE!

 Made on the stove, this recipe needs YOUR PERSON with you the whole time.

 1. To the saucepan, add the pitted cherries, white sugar, freshly squeezed orange juice and orange zest. Place the saucepan on your stove. Turn the stove to medium heat and bring this mixture to a simmering boil. Using the mixing spoon, MIX until the sugar disappears. Turn the heat to low and simmer for 10 minutes.

 2. To the small bowl, add the cornstarch and cold water. Using the whisk, WHISK until the cornstarch disappears. This white liquid is called a slurry!

 3. Add the slurry to the saucepan with the cherries. Using the mixing spoon, MIX in the slurry. Turn up the heat on the stove to medium. Bring the mixture to a boil and allow to boil for 30 seconds while mixing.

4. Using the oven mitts, carefully remove the saucepan from the heat. Pour the cherry compote into the medium heatproof bowl.

 5. Using the spatula, SCRAPE down the sides and bottom of the saucepan, adding every last drop to the bowl.

6. Using the fork, gently mush the cherries against the side of the bowl, breaking up any big pieces.

7. Let the compote cool completely in the bowl. BING!

   **Save for later?** Store the compote in an airtight container in the fridge for up to 10 days.

**FUN FACT:**
 Cherries have some thorny relatives! They actually belong to the rose family. Maybe the poem should go: Cherries are red, violets are blue . . .

 Continue your baking adventure in **Cupcakeland** (page 63)! There you can try making yummy cupcakes to fill! Our favorite flavor match is **Banana-nana Cupcakes** (page 71)!

# Jam Out Berry Jam!

## Makes about 2 cups (photo on page 44)

This recipe is totally our jam! Like, it's really OUR jam. Packed with big berry flavor and so easy to make, you'll want to put it on more than just desserts. Your breakfast toast will thank you.

 Get Ready...

| TOOLS |
|---|
| ☐ Measuring cups and spoons |
| ☐ Medium saucepan |
| ☐ Mixing spoon |
| ☐ Oven mitts |
| ☐ Medium heatproof bowl |

| INGREDIENTS | |
|---|---|
| 2 cups | your favorite berries, fresh or frozen |
| ⅓ cup | white sugar |
| 1 tablespoon | freshly squeezed lemon juice |
| ½ teaspoon | lemon zest |

**There's more to explore!**
Go to the **Information Booth** on page 7 to discover more about boiling points.

# ... BAKE!

 Made on the stove, this recipe needs YOUR PERSON with you the whole time.

1. To the saucepan, add the berries, white sugar, freshly squeezed lemon juice and lemon zest. Place the saucepan on your stove. Turn the stove to medium heat and bring this mixture to a boil.

2. Once it's boiling, turn down the heat to medium-low and cook the jam. Using the mixing spoon, MIX it every 3 minutes. Cook until the jam has thickened. It will shrink to half its original size, about 10 minutes.

Yolk yolk yolk! Why was the strawberry late for school?

It was stuck in a traffic JAM!

3. Using the oven mitts, carefully remove the saucepan from the heat. Slowly and carefully pour the jam into the medium heatproof bowl and let it cool completely.

**Save for later?** Store the jam in an airtight container in the fridge for up to 3 weeks.

Continue your baking adventure in **Cookieland** (page 37), **Cakeland** (page 175) or **Donutland** (page 153)! Try baking up a batch of cookies and making jammy cookie sandwiches! Our favorite flavor match is L M N O ... **Peanut Butter Cookies** (page 45). Or try using this delicious jam as a sweet filling for the **Pillow Donuts** (page 158) or **Pink Cake** (page 177).

# Princess Banana Lips

## Makes about 4 cups (photo on page 75)

When a pastry cream is mixed with fluffy whipped cream it becomes a princess cream. When a princess cream is mixed with a bright banana flavor, it becomes Princess Banana Lips. Velvety smooth and lick-your-lips delicious, she's got a lot of a-peel. Two saucepans are a must for this recipe.

 Get Ready...

| TOOLS |
|-------|
| ☐ Measuring cups and spoons |
| ☐ 2 small bowls |
| ☐ 2 medium saucepans |
| ☐ Whisk |
| ☐ Oven mitts |
| ☐ Mixing spoon |
| ☐ Sifter |
| ☐ Large heatproof bowl |
| ☐ Plastic wrap |
| ☐ Electric mixer |
| ☐ Spatula |

| INGREDIENTS | |
|-------------|--|
| 1 sheet | gelatin |
| ½ cup | water |
| 6 tablespoons | light brown sugar |
| 4 | large egg yolks |
| 3 tablespoons | cornstarch |
| ⅛ teaspoon | table salt |
| 2 cups | whole milk |
| ¼ cup | salted butter |
| 1 teaspoon | banana extract |
| ½ cup | whipping cream |

**There's more to explore!**
Go to the **Information Booth** on page 7 to discover more about separating eggs, boiling points and whipping peaks!

# . . . BAKE!

 Made on the stove, this recipe needs YOUR PERSON with you the whole time.

1. To 1 small bowl, add the sheet of gelatin and water. Set this bowl to the side to let the gelatin soften.

2. To 1 saucepan, off the heat, add the light brown sugar, egg yolks, cornstarch and salt. Using the whisk, WHISK until everything comes together.

3. To the other saucepan, add the milk. Place this saucepan on your stove. Turn the stove to medium-low heat and bring the milk to a simmer.

4. Using the oven mitts, carefully pour the warm milk into the saucepan with the eggy mixture.

5. WHISK until everything is combined.

6. Remove the sheet of gelatin from the bowl (it should be soft and slimy) and add it to the saucepan with the eggy mixture.

7. Place the saucepan on your stove. Turn the stove to medium heat and bring the mixture to a simmering boil. Using the mixing spoon, MIX until the mixture thickens, about 5 minutes.

8. Using the oven mitts, carefully remove the saucepan from the heat. MIX in the butter and banana extract.

9. Place the sifter on top of the large heatproof bowl. Pour the thickened cream through it. This should get rid of any unwanted lumps or bumps!

10. Lay a large sheet of plastic wrap over the bowl and press down so the plastic wrap is touching the cream. Pop the bowl of cream in your fridge to chill for 4 hours.

. . .

11. After 4 hours, to the other small bowl, add the whipping cream. Using the electric mixer, BEAT on medium-high speed until medium peaks form.

12. Using the spatula, FOLD in the whipped cream to the cooled banana cream. Continue to FOLD until they're just mixed together.

Save for later? Store the cream in an airtight container in the fridge for up to 3 days.

 Continue your baking adventure in Cupcakeland (page 63), where this filling is just perfect for our Vanilla Cloud-Cakes (page 73)!

# Vanilla Ice Scream (GF)

### Makes about 6 cups (photo on page 50)

AAAAAAAAGGGHHHHHHHH! I SCREAM, YOU SCREAM, WE ALL SCREAM FOR ICE CREAM!
Especially ice cream that has just three ingredients and doesn't need an ice cream machine to make it!
AAAAAAAAGGGHHHHHHHH!

## Get Ready...

| TOOLS |
|---|
| ☐ Measuring cups and spoons |
| ☐ Medium bowl |
| ☐ Whisk |
| ☐ Large bowl |
| ☐ Electric mixer |
| ☐ Spatula |
| ☐ Loaf pan |
| ☐ Plastic wrap |

| INGREDIENTS | |
|---|---|
| 1 can (6.6 ounces/ 195 ml) | sweetened condensed milk |
| 1 teaspoon | vanilla bean paste |
| 2 cups | whipping cream |

**There's more to explore!**
Go to the **Information Booth** on page 7 to
discover more about whipping peaks.

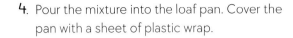

# ... BAKE!

1. To the medium bowl, add the sweetened condensed milk and vanilla bean paste. Using the whisk, WHISK until everything is combined. Set this bowl to the side.

2. To the large bowl, add the whipping cream. Using the electric mixer, BEAT on high speed until it reaches soft peaks.

3. Add the whipped cream to the bowl with the condensed milk. Using the spatula, FOLD it in, lifting the condensed milk from the bottom of the bowl and bringing it to the top.

4. Pour the mixture into the loaf pan. Cover the pan with a sheet of plastic wrap.

5. Pop the pan of ice cream in your freezer to firm up for 8-12 hours, and ideally overnight. Go ahead and scream! You just made ice cream!! AAAAAAAAGGGHHHHHHHH!

**Save for later?** Store the ice cream in an airtight container in the freezer for up to 5 days.

Continue your baking adventure in **Cookieland** (page 37)! There you can try making ice cream cookie sandwiches! Our favorite flavor match is **Gingerbread Molasses Cookies** (page 51) or **Chocolate Fudge Cookies** (page 57)!

# FROSTINGS

These recipes are the tops! Here you can explore six great recipes to slather over the top of your baked goods or squish in the middle. Now let your imagination fly!

# Nutty Peanut Butter Frosting (GF)

### Makes about 2 cups (photo on page 181)

We're nutty about this ultra-creamy frosting! To balance the sweetness, we recommend you use natural peanut butter. This frosting is lip-smacking good!

## ☑ Get Ready...

### TOOLS

- ☐ Measuring cups and spoons
- ☐ Sifter
- ☐ Large bowl
- ☐ Electric mixer
- ☐ Spatula

**There's more to explore!**
Go to the **Information Booth** on page 7 to discover more about room temperature.

### INGREDIENTS

| | |
|---|---|
| 1 cup | cream cheese, at room temperature |
| ½ cup | salted butter, at room temperature |
| ½ cup | natural smooth peanut butter |
| ½ teaspoon | vanilla extract |
| 1½ cups | powdered sugar, sifted |

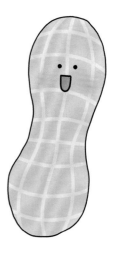

# . . . BAKE!

1. To the large bowl, add the cream cheese and butter. Using the electric mixer, BEAT on medium speed until the mixture is smooth, about 2 minutes.

2. Using the spatula, SCRAPE down the sides and bottom of the bowl.

3. Add the peanut butter and vanilla extract. BEAT on medium speed for 30 seconds more. Add ½ cup of the sifted powdered sugar. With the mixer on the lowest speed, BEAT for 20 seconds.

4. Using the spatula, SCRAPE down the sides and bottom of the bowl. Repeat with another ½ cup of powdered sugar. Continue to BEAT and SCRAPE until all the powdered sugar is added.

5. Increase the speed on the mixer to high. BEAT until the frosting is light and fluffy, about 2 minutes. Go nuts!

**Save for later?** Store the frosting in an airtight container in the fridge for up to 1 week.

Continue your baking adventure in **Cakeland** (page 175). There you can try making a yummy cake to frost! Our favorite flavor match is **Disappearing Chocolate Cake** (page 179)! This frosting is super cute when piped with a basket weave tip (page 33) to look like a peanut shell!

# Chocolate Milky Way Frosting (GF)

### Makes about 3 cups (photo on page 69)

This chocolate frosting is creamy and delicious. In fact, it tastes OUT OF THIS WORLD!
Our trick to making it silky smooth is to keep it on the stove until the sugar has melted completely.
Watch it carefully!

 ☑ Get Ready...

## TOOLS

- ☐ Measuring cups and spoons
- ☐ Spouted measuring cup
- ☐ Whisk
- ☐ Medium saucepan
- ☐ Spatula
- ☐ Oven mitts
- ☐ Mixing spoon
- ☐ Large heatproof bowl
- ☐ Electric mixer

## INGREDIENTS

| | |
|---|---|
| 1¼ cups | whipping cream |
| ⅓ cup | sour cream |
| ½ cup | salted butter |
| 1½ cups | white sugar |
| 1¼ cups | cocoa powder, sifted |
| 1½ teaspoons | vanilla extract |

**There's more to explore!**
Go to the **Information Booth** on page 7 to discover more about sifting.

# . . . BAKE!

 1. To the spouted measuring cup, add the whipping cream and sour cream. Using the whisk, WHISK until everything is combined. Set this measuring cup to the side.

 2. FIND YOUR PERSON To the saucepan, add the butter. Place the saucepan on your stove over low heat and gently melt the butter. Add the white sugar, cocoa powder and cream mixture. WHISK until everything is combined.

 3. Turn the heat up to medium and continue to WHISK until the frosting is smooth and the sugar has dissolved, about 5 minutes.

 4. FIND YOUR PERSON Using the oven mitts, carefully remove the saucepan from the heat.

 5. Using the mixing spoon, MIX in the vanilla extract.

 6. Carefully pour the frosting into the large heatproof bowl. SCRAPE down the sides and bottom of the saucepan, adding every last drop to the bowl.

7. Pop the bowl of frosting in your fridge to chill for about 1 hour.

. . .

 8. Using the electric mixer, BEAT on medium-high speed until the frosting fluffs up, about 2 minutes. You're a star!

**Save for later?** Store the frosting in an airtight container in the fridge for up to 1 week.

Continue your baking adventure in **Cupcakeland** (page 63)! There you can try baking up a batch of cupcakes to slather this frosting all over. Our favorite flavor match is **Chocolate Ker-Pow Cupcakes** (page 67)! To dial up the chocolate fun, we love taking a trip to Toppings to add **Chocolate Bar Curls** (page 138) to decorate this chocolate frosting.

# Buttercream Bomb (GF)

### Makes about 2 cups (photo on page 182)

This recipe for vanilla buttercream is THE BOMB. Made with just four simple ingredients, it comes together effortlessly. We use salted butter, as it cuts the sweetness perfectly! Mind. Blown.

 Get Ready...

| TOOLS |
|---|
| ☐ Measuring cups and spoons |
| ☐ Sifter |
| ☐ Large bowl |
| ☐ Electric mixer |
| ☐ Spatula |

| INGREDIENTS | |
|---|---|
| 1 cup | salted butter, at room temperature |
| 3½ cups | powdered sugar, sifted |
| ¼ cup | table cream |
| 1 tablespoon | vanilla extract |

**There's more to explore!**
Go to the *Information Booth* on page 7 to discover more about sifting and room temperature.

# . . . BAKE!

1. To the large bowl, add the butter. Using the electric mixer, BEAT on medium-high speed until it's light and fluffy, about 2 minutes.

2. Add 1 cup of the powdered sugar. With the mixer on the lowest speed, BEAT for 20 seconds.

3. Using the spatula, SCRAPE down the sides and bottom of the bowl.

4. Repeat step 2 and 3, adding the powdered sugar in 2 more additions, until it is all added.

5. Add the cream and vanilla extract. BEAT on medium-high speed until the mixture is light and fluffy, about 2 minutes. BAM!

**Save for later?** Store the buttercream in an airtight container for up to 2 weeks.

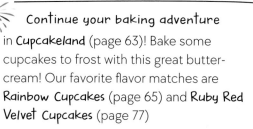

Continue your baking adventure in **Cupcakeland** (page 63)! Bake some cupcakes to frost with this great butter-cream! Our favorite flavor matches are **Rainbow Cupcakes** (page 65) and **Ruby Red Velvet Cupcakes** (page 77)

# Marvelous Mallow Frosting

### Makes about 2 cups (photo on page 187)

This marshmallow frosting is made with vegan marshmallows and it's marvelous! Perfectly sweet with a light fluffy texture, it's sure to be a favorite for all your vegan baking creations! This recipe needs a little more mixing muscle than most other recipes in this book. A stand mixer is a must!

 Get Ready...

## TOOLS

- ☐ Measuring cups and spoons
- ☐ Sifter
- ☐ Small microwave-safe bowl
- ☐ Stand mixer with whisk attachment

**There's more to explore!**
Go to the **Information Booth** on page 7 to discover more about sifting.

## INGREDIENTS

| | |
|---|---|
| ½ cup | vegan marshmallows |
| 6 tablespoons | vegan butter at room temperature |
| 2½ cups | powdered sugar, sifted |
| 2 tablespoons | coconut cream |
| 1 teaspoon | freshly squeezed lemon juice |
| 1 teaspoon | vanilla extract |

# . . . BAKE!

 Made using the microwave and a stand mixer, this recipe needs YOUR PERSON with you the whole time.

1. To the small microwave-safe bowl, add the vegan marshmallows.

2. Soften the marshmallows in the microwave for 20 seconds.

3. To the bowl of your stand mixer, add the softened marshmallows, vegan butter, 1 cup of the powdered sugar and 1 tablespoon of the coconut cream. Beat on low speed until everything is mixed, about 10 seconds.

4. Add the remaining 1 tablespoon of coconut cream, the lemon juice, vanilla extract and 1 cup of the powdered sugar. Beat on low speed for 20 seconds.

5. Add the remaining ½ cup of the powdered sugar. Beat on low speed until everything is combined. Increase the speed on the mixer to high. Beat for another 30 seconds to make it super fluffy.

6. Let the frosting rest in the fridge for 10 minutes before using.

    **Save for later?** Store the frosting in an airtight container in the fridge for up to 2 weeks.

**Continue your baking adventure** in **Cakeland** (page 175)! There you can make a vegan cake to decorate with this frosting. Our favorite flavor match is **Caramel Apple Cake** (page 185).

# Fluffy Cream Cheese Frosting

### Makes about 2 cups (photo on page 81)

This frosting is EVERYTHING! It's tangy and sweet and irresistibly good.
We still squabble over who gets to lick the spoon! I do, I do!

 Get Ready...

| TOOLS |
|---|
| ☐ Measuring cups and spoons |
| ☐ Sifter |
| ☐ Large bowl |
| ☐ Electric mixer |
| ☐ Spatula |

| INGREDIENTS | |
|---|---|
| 1 cup | cream cheese, at room temperature |
| ¼ cup + 2 tablespoons | butter, at room temperature |
| 2½ cups | powdered sugar, sifted |
| 1 teaspoon | vanilla extract |

**There's more to explore!**

Go to the **Information Booth** on page 7 to discover more about room temperature and sifting.

# . . . BAKE!

 1. To the large bowl, add the cream cheese and butter. Using the electric mixer, BEAT on medium speed until the mixture is smooth, about 1 minute.

 2. Add half of the powdered sugar. With the mixer on the lowest speed, BEAT for 20 seconds.

 3. Using the spatula, SCRAPE down the sides and bottom of the bowl.

 4. Add the rest of the powdered sugar. With the mixer on the lowest speed, BEAT for 20 seconds.

 5. Add the vanilla extract. On medium-high speed, BEAT until the frosting is super fluffy, 2 more minutes.

**Save for later?** Store the frosting in an airtight container in the fridge for up to 1 week.

 **Continue your baking adventure** in **Cakeland** (page 175) or **Cupcakeland** (page 63)! There you can try making a tasty cake or cupcake to slather this frosting all over! Our favorite flavor match is **Lemony Olive Oil Cake** (page 191) or **Cinnamon Hug Cupcakes** (page 79)!

# Strawberry Patch Frosting

### Makes about 2 cups (photo on page 176)

This frosting is the best! Sweetly pink and bursting with bright, bold, berry flavor!

 Get Ready...

| TOOLS |
|---|
| ☐ Measuring cups and spoons |
| ☐ Sifter |
| ☐ Small bowl |
| ☐ Large bowl |
| ☐ Electric mixer |
| ☐ Spatula |

| INGREDIENTS | |
|---|---|
| 2 tablespoons | strawberry jelly powder |
| ¼ cup | boiling water |
| ¼ cup + 2 tablespoons | salted butter, at room temperature |
| 2½ cups | powdered sugar, sifted |
| 2 tablespoons | table cream |

**There's more to explore!**
Go to the *Information Booth* on page 7 to discover more about sifting and room temperature.

# . . . BAKE!

1. FIND YOUR PERSON To the small bowl, add the jelly powder and boiling water. Set this bowl to the side and let it cool for 5 minutes.

2. To the large bowl, add the cooled jelly mixture, butter and 2 cups of the powdered sugar. Using the electric mixer, BEAT on low speed until everything is combined, about 10 seconds. Add 1 tablespoon of the cream. BEAT for 10 seconds more to fluff it up.

3. Using the spatula, SCRAPE down the sides and bottom of the bowl.

4. Add the remaining 1 tablespoon of cream and the remaining ½ cup of powdered sugar. BEAT on low speed for 10 seconds. Crank up the speed to high and BEAT for 30 seconds more to make it fluffy. The berry best!

**Save for later?** Store the frosting in an airtight container in the fridge for up to 1 week.

Continue your baking adventure in **Cakeland** (page 175) or **Cookieland** (page 37)! There you can try baking a yummy cake or cookie to frost with this pretty frosting! Our favorite flavor matches are **Pink Cake** (page 177) and **Goldilocks's Oatmeal Cookies** (page 53)!

# GLAZES AND MORE

Drizzles, icing and glazes are great! They are usually thinner than frostings so they are perfect for dripping, dipping and dunking your desserts. No matter how you use them, they will ROCK your boat!

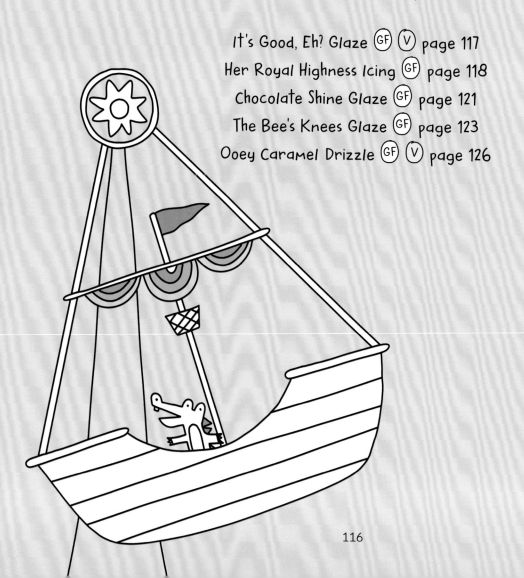

# It's Good, Eh? Glaze

### Makes about 1/2 cup (photo on page 168)

Pure Canadian maple syrup is a must for this recipe! It's really good, eh?! This glaze comes together in a matter of seconds—it's that easy. If you're just planning on frosting the top of your dessert, add a little more powdered sugar to thicken it up! Is your glaze too thick? Add ¼ teaspoon of water to thin it out!

 Get Ready...

| TOOLS |
|---|
| ☐ Measuring cups and spoons |
| ☐ Sifter |
| ☐ Small bowl |
| ☐ Whisk |

| INGREDIENTS | |
|---|---|
| 1 cup | powdered sugar, sifted |
| 2 tablespoons | pure maple syrup |
| 1 tablespoon | non-dairy milk |

**There's more to explore!**
Go to the **Information Booth** on page 7 to discover more about sifting.

## ... BAKE!

 1. To the small bowl, add the powdered sugar, maple syrup and milk. Using the whisk, WHISK until the mixture is lump-free. You're done!

**Save for later?** Store the glaze in an airtight container in the fridge for up to 2 weeks. Gently warm in the microwave or stove before next use.

 Continue your baking adventure in **Donutland** (page 153)! Make some delish donuts for dipping or dunking into this glaze! Our favorite flavor matches are **Sugar and Spice and Everything Nice Donuts** (page 169), **I'm Coconuts for You! Donuts** (page 164), or **Chocolate Date Donuts** (page 161).

# Her Royal Highness Icing

### Makes about 1 cup (photo on page 173)

This is our fun take on royal icing. We love this recipe 'cause you don't have to wait hours and hours and hours for it to dry—meaning you get to eat your iced cookies, donuts and cakes sooner! Hooray!

 Get Ready...

### TOOLS

- ☐ Measuring cups and spoons
- ☐ Sifter
- ☐ Large bowl
- ☐ Whisk
- ☐ Small spoon

### INGREDIENTS

| | |
|---|---|
| 3 cups | powdered sugar, sifted |
| 2 tablespoons | whole milk |
| 2 tablespoons | light corn syrup |
| ¾ teaspoon | vanilla extract |
| Water for thinning | |
| Food coloring, gel or liquid, optional (see page 207) | |

**There's more to explore!**
Go to the **Information Booth** on page 7 to discover more about sifting, and the **Coloring Box** on page 35 for color inspiration!

# . . . BAKE!

 1. To the large bowl, add the powdered sugar, milk, light corn syrup and vanilla extract. Using the whisk, WHISK until the icing is in large clumps. Add 1 teaspoon of water and WHISK until everything is combined.

 2. Continue to add water, 1 teaspoon at a time, and WHISK until the icing is a smooth, thick paste.

3. Add the food coloring of your choice. Using the small spoon, stir until everything is blended. Excellent!

Save for later? Store the icing in an airtight container in the fridge for up to 3 days. WHISK it before you use it.

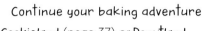

Continue your baking adventure in **Cookieland** (page 37) or **Donutland** (page 153)! Try making some fabulous cookies or donuts to decorate with this icing! Our favorite flavor match is **Sugar Sugar Sugar Cookies** (page 59) or **Baked Strawberries and Cream Donuts** (page 171)!

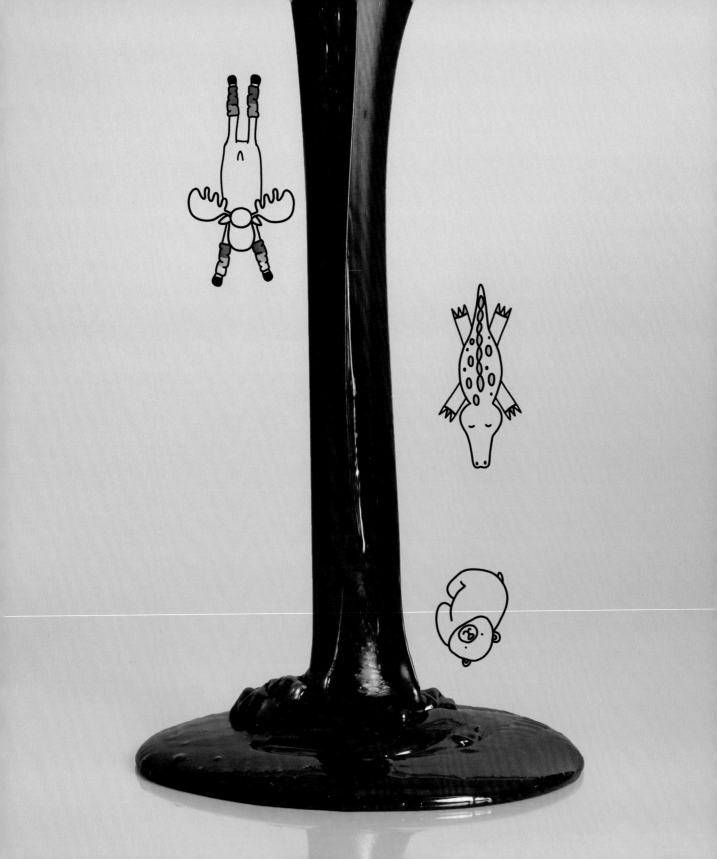

# Chocolate Shine Glaze (GF)

### Makes about 3/4 cup (photo on page 157)

Shiny and sweet, this glaze is a treat! We love it so much we often double the recipe for double the shine.

 Get Ready...

## TOOLS

- ☐ Measuring cups and spoons
- ☐ Small saucepan
- ☐ Mixing spoon
- ☐ Oven mitts
- ☐ Medium heatproof bowl
- ☐ Spatula

## INGREDIENTS

| | |
|---|---|
| 1 tablespoon | salted butter |
| ¼ cup | light or dark corn syrup |
| ½ cup | semisweet chocolate chips |
| ½ teaspoon | vanilla extract |

**There's more to explore!**
Go to the **Information Booth** on page 7 to discover more about boiling points.

# . . . BAKE!

 **Made on the stove, this recipe needs** YOUR PERSON **with you the whole time.**

 1. To the small saucepan, add the butter, corn syrup and chocolate chips. Place the saucepan on your stove on medium heat. Using the mixing spoon, MIX as the butter and chocolate chips melt.

 2. Once melted, using the oven mitts, carefully remove the saucepan from the heat. MIX in the vanilla extract.

3. Carefully pour the chocolate glaze into the heatproof bowl.

 4. Using the spatula, SCRAPE down the sides and bottom of the saucepan, adding every last drop to the bowl. So shiny!

**Save for later?** Store the glaze in an airtight container in the fridge for up to 10 days. Gently reheat it in the microwave or in a saucepan on the stove before you use it.

**Continue your baking adventure** in **Cakeland** (page 175) or **Donutland** (page 153)! There you can try baking up a great cake or donut to drizzle this chocolate glaze over! Our favorite flavor matches are **Chipper Chocolate Chip Cake** (page 189). or **Shoe-nuts** (page 154)

# The Bee's Knees Glaze (GF)

Makes about 3/4 cup (photo on page 156)

Sticky and sweet and a breeze to make, this glaze is terrific! It's our runniest glaze, and it's best enjoyed when you completely dunk your baked goods in it and then allow the glaze to harden. It's so good, it's THE BEE'S KNEES.

 Get Ready...

## TOOLS

- ☐ Measuring cups and spoons
- ☐ Medium saucepan
- ☐ Whisk
- ☐ Sifter
- ☐ Medium heatproof bowl
- ☐ Oven mitts

## INGREDIENTS

| | |
|---|---|
| ¼ cup | salted butter |
| ½ cup | honey |
| ⅛ teaspoon | ground cardamom |
| ⅛ teaspoon | cornstarch |

**There's more to explore!**
Go to the **Information Booth** on page 7 to discover more about boiling points.

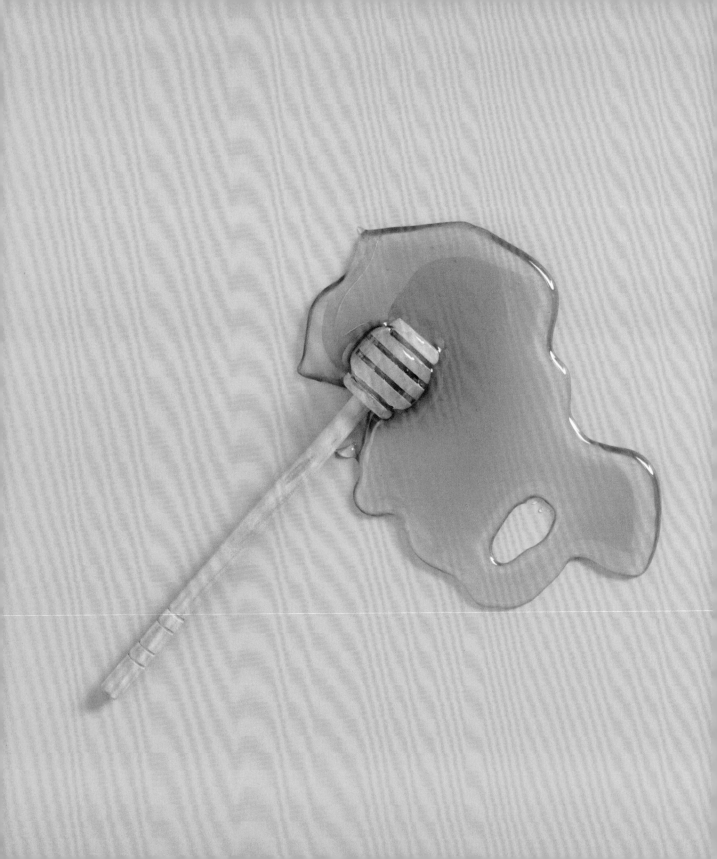

# . . . BAKE!

 **Made on the stove, this recipe needs** YOUR PERSON **with you the whole time.**

1. To the saucepan, add the butter. Place the saucepan on your stove. Turn the stove to low heat and gently melt the butter. Once the butter is melted, add the honey, ground cardamom and cornstarch. Turn up the heat to medium. Bring the mixture to a boil. Watch it carefully, as it won't take long.

 2. Once it's boiling, using the whisk, WHISK for 30 seconds.

3. Place the sifter on top of the heatproof bowl. Using the oven mitts, slowly and carefully pour the glaze through the sifter into the bowl. Allow the glaze to cool for 5 minutes. Isn't that sweet?!

   **Save for later?** Store the glaze in an airtight container in the fridge for up to 5 days. Gently reheat it in the microwave or in a saucepan on the stove before you use it.

 Continue your baking adventure in **Donutland** (page 153)! There you can try making some divine donuts to dunk in this sticky glaze. Our favorite flavor match is **Shoe-nuts** (page 154)!

# Ooey Caramel Drizzle

### Makes about 1 cup (photo page 187)

This dreamy drizzle is so rich and delicious AND it's vegan!
It gets its lusciousness from coconut cream. Va va voom!

 Get Ready...

| TOOLS |
|---|
| ☐ Measuring cups and spoons |
| ☐ Small saucepan |
| ☐ Whisk |
| ☐ Oven mitts |
| ☐ Medium heatproof bowl |

| INGREDIENTS | |
|---|---|
| 2 tablespoons | vegan butter |
| 1 cup | light brown sugar |
| ¼ cup | coconut cream |
| 1 teaspoon | light or dark corn syrup |
| 1 teaspoon | vanilla extract |
| ⅛ teaspoon | table salt |

**There's more to explore!**
Go to the **Information Booth** on page 7 to
discover more about boiling points.

# . . . BAKE!

Made on the stove, this recipe needs YOUR PERSON with you the whole time.

1. To the small saucepan, add the vegan butter, brown sugar, coconut cream, corn syrup, vanilla extract and salt. Using the whisk, WHISK until everything is combined.

2. Place the saucepan on your stove. Turn the stove to medium-high heat. Cook the mixture until it begins to foam with large bubbles. Once it's foaming, turn the heat down to medium-low.

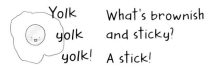

Yolk yolk yolk! What's brownish and sticky? A stick!

3. Cook for 6 minutes, WHISK-ing every 2 minutes.

4. Using the oven mitts, carefully remove the saucepan from the heat. Slowly and carefully pour the caramel into the heatproof bowl. Let the caramel cool for 10 minutes before using.

   **Save for later?** Not with this recipe! The caramel should be used within 2 hours of making it.

Continue your baking adventure in **Cakeland** (page 175)! There you can try baking a cake and drizzling it with this gorgeous glaze! Our favorite flavor match is **Caramel Apple Cake** (page 185).

# TOPPINGS

Yippee! If you're reading this part, you're ready to add some shimmer and shine to your finished baking creation! Here you'll find all sorts of fun and easy recipes for toppings. Let the sprinkles fly!

# Cloud Cream (GF)

## Makes about 2 1/2 cups (photo on page 4)

Light and creamy and simple to make, this sweetened whipped cream
is perfect for snuggling up to any dessert.

 Get Ready...

| TOOLS |
| --- |
| ☐ Measuring cups and spoons |
| ☐ Large bowl |
| ☐ Electric mixer |

| INGREDIENTS | |
| --- | --- |
| 1 cup | whipping cream |
| 1 tablespoon | white sugar |
| ½ teaspoon | vanilla extract |

 **There's more to explore!**
Go to the **Information Booth** on page 7 to
discover more about whipping peaks.

 ... BAKE!

 1. To the large bowl, add the whipping cream,
white sugar and vanilla extract. Using the
electric mixer, BEAT on high speed until soft
peaks form.

   **Save for later?** Store the cream in an airtight
   container in the fridge and use within 2 hours
   of making it.

**Continue your baking adventure**
here in **Wonderpark** (page 83)! Try topping
one of the delicious hot chocolates with
this cream! Our favorite flavor match is **Hot
Cocoa** (page 148).

# FUN-dant

## Makes 1 1/2 cups of fun! (photo on page 4)

You'll have so much FUN making this dessert topping and then coloring it and molding it into all sorts of FUN shapes! There are so many FUN colors you can make too. We dyed ours 10 different colors and shaped it into a rainbow!

## Get Ready...

| TOOLS |
|---|
| ☐ Measuring cups and spoons |
| ☐ Sifter |
| ☐ Extra-large glass bowl |
| ☐ Spatula |
| ☐ Large pot with handle |
| ☐ Oven mitts |
| ☐ Plastic wrap |
| ☐ Small bowl |
| ☐ Toothpicks |

| INGREDIENTS | |
|---|---|
| 3½ cups | powdered sugar, sifted |
| 1 (8.8 ounces/250 g) bag | mini marshmallows |
| 2 tablespoons | water |
| 1 tablespoon | coconut oil, for your hands |
| Food coloring gel, optional (see page 207) | |

### There's more to explore!

Go to the *Information Booth* on page 7 to discover more about sifting, kneading and creating different colors.

# . . . BAKE!

1. Place 3 cups of the powdered sugar in the extra-large glass bowl, making the sugar into a hill.

2. Using the spatula, dig a big hole (about the size of a baseball) in the center of the powdered sugar. This hole is called a well.

3. FIND YOUR PERSON To the large pot, add the mini marshmallows and water. Place the pot on your stove. Turn the stove to medium heat. Using the oven mitts, carefully hold onto the pot's handle with 1 hand.

4. With your other hand, take your spatula and quickly FOLD in the marshmallows until they're melted, about 5 minutes.

5. FIND YOUR PERSON Carefully remove the pot from the heat and empty the melted marsh-mallows into the well of powdered sugar.

6. Using the spatula, SCRAPE down the sides and bottom of the pot, adding every last drop to the bowl.

7. FOLD the powdered sugar and the hot marshmallow mixture together. It's going to be sticky and get stickier! Continue to FOLD for 1 minute more to help it cool down.

8. Rub your HANDS with the coconut oil (just like you would lotion)! This will help keep the sticky marshmallow goop off your hands. Carefully touch the mixture with your

pointer finger to test its coolness. It should be warm to the touch but not hot. If it's warm enough to touch, sprinkle with the remaining ½ cup of powdered sugar.

9. Using your HANDS, squish and smush the mixture (it will be very crumbly) until the mixture forms into a smooth ball, about 5 minutes.

10. Wrap the FUN-dant in plastic wrap and let it sit on the counter for 1 hour.

. . .

11. If you want to color the FUN-dant, break a piece off and place it in the small bowl. Using a toothpick, dip the toothpick in your desired color of food coloring gel and smear the toothpick on the piece of FUN-dant.

12. Using your HANDS, work the color in by mushing and rolling the FUN-dant between your fingers. Yay! You're ready to play and eat!

Save for later? Wrap colored FUN-dant in plastic wrap and store in an airtight bag in your pantry for up to 4 weeks.

Continue your baking adventure in Cakeland (page 175)! There you can try baking a cake for your funny FUN-dant to sit on! Our favorite flavor match is Confetti Cake (page 183).

# Toasted Coconut

### Makes 1 cup (photo on page 166)

We double dare you to find something in Baking Wonderland that toasted coconut doesn't taste good on . . . We haven't found it yet!

 Get Ready...

| TOOLS |
|---|
| ☐ Measuring cups and spoons |
| ☐ Medium saucepan |
| ☐ Mixing spoon |
| ☐ Oven mitts |
| ☐ Medium bowl |

| INGREDIENTS | |
|---|---|
| 1 cup | sweetened coconut flakes |

## . . . BAKE!

 **Made on the stove, this recipe needs** YOUR PERSON **with you the whole time.**

1. To the saucepan, add the coconut flakes. Place the saucepan on the stove. Turn the stove to medium heat.

 2. Using the mixing spoon, MIX the coconut until it turns light brown, about 3-5 minutes.

3. Using the oven mitts, carefully remove the saucepan from the stove and tip the toasted coconut immediately into the bowl to cool.

**Save for later?** Store toasted coconut in an airtight container in your pantry for up to 4 weeks.

**Continue your baking adventure** in **Donutland** (page 153)! There you can sprinkle this topping on one of our yummy donuts. Our favorite flavor match is **I'm Coconuts for You! Donuts** (page 164).

# Chocolate Potato Chips and Pretzels

Makes 2 cups (photo on page 188)

Y-E-S to the ultimate sweet and salty combination!!

 Get Ready...

| TOOLS |
| --- |
| ☐ Measuring cups and spoons |
| ☐ Cookie sheet |
| ☐ Parchment paper |
| ☐ Medium microwave-safe bowl |
| ☐ Whisk |
| ☐ Oven mitts |

| INGREDIENTS | |
| --- | --- |
| 1 cup | semisweet chocolate chips |
| 2 cups | plain potato chips (the rippled ones work great!) or salted pretzels |

## ...BAKE!

1. Cover the cookie sheet with parchment paper. Set the cookie sheet to the side.

2. FIND YOUR PERSON To the microwave-safe bowl, add the chocolate chips. Melt them in the microwave on high for 15 seconds. Using the whisk, WHISK them. Continue to microwave them for 15 seconds at a time until melted, about 1 minute in total, WHISK-ing after every 15 seconds.

3. FIND YOUR PERSON Using the oven mitts, carefully remove the hot bowl of melted chocolate from the microwave.

4. Working with 1 potato chip or pretzel at a time, dip it into the bowl of chocolate (but don't let it go!). Swirl it around in the melted chocolate. Be careful! It will be hot! Once it's coated in chocolate, place on the prepared cookie sheet to harden.

Continue your baking adventure in **Cakeland** (page 175)! There you can try these as a salty and sweet, crunchy topping on one of the cakes! Our favorite flavor match is **Chipper Chocolate Chip Cake** (page 189).

Sugar Berries
(page 135)

Fluffy Cream
Cheese Frosting
(page 111)

Chocolate Moose
(page 87)

Chocolate
Ker-Pow
Cupcakes
(page 67)

Marvelous
Mallow Frosting
(page 109)

Rainbow
Cupcakes
(page 65)

# Sugar Berries

## Makes 1 cup

Add a pop of fresh berry flavor and a burst of color to your dessert with these sugared berries. We love using raspberries but you can make them with the berry of your choice. How sweet?!

 Get Ready...

| TOOLS |
| --- |
| ☐ Measuring cups and spoons |
| ☐ 2 small bowls |
| ☐ Cooling rack |

| INGREDIENTS | |
| --- | --- |
| ¼ cup | pure maple syrup |
| 1 cup | white sugar |
| 1 cup | fresh berries |

## ...BAKE!

1. To 1 small bowl, add the maple syrup.

2. To the other small bowl, add the white sugar.

3. Using your HANDS, quickly dip a berry into the maple syrup so it's lightly covered in syrup on all sides but not dripping.

4. Next, roll it in the sugar bowl until it's sparkly all over.

5. Place on the cooling rack and let dry for 1 hour before using to decorate. So pretty!

**Continue your baking adventure** in Cupcakeland (page 63)! There you can use these as a berry nice topping on one of the cupcakes! Our favorite flavor match is **Ruby Red Velvet Cupcakes** (page 77) with **Buttercream Bomb** frosting (page 107) and a ton of sprinkles.

Cinnamon Sugar
(page 139)

Strawberry Fans
(page 138)

# Strawberry Fans

Using the butter knife, slice off the leafy tops of the strawberries. Place a strawberry, top side down, on a cutting board. Now slice down the strawberry until you almost cut through it but not quite. Repeat until the strawberry has several cuts, all running in the same direction. Using your thumbs, carefully fan out the strawberry slices as if you were fanning out a hand of cards. It will take practice to get it just right! But the good news is you can eat the ones that don't work!

# Chocolate Bar Curls

The easiest way to get gorgeous curly chocolate curls is to take a vegetable peeler and run it down the side of your favorite hard chocolate bar. Collect the curls and decorate!

# Stuff

If you can eat it, you can use it to decorate! Finding neat-looking edible stuff around the kitchen is probably one of our favorite ways to decorate our desserts! Cotton candy? Ok! Popcorn? Why not?! We promise you, whatever your dessert looks like, we already love it—it was made by you! Use your imagination when it comes to decorating and play with your food!

# Sugar Snow

Make it look like your desserts have just been dusted with a light powder of snow! Place a sifter on top of a medium bowl. Add about ½ cup of powdered sugar to the sifter. Gently lift the sifter up with one hand and hover it over the baked goods you are decorating (make sure they have fully cooled first). With your other hand, bang the sides of the sifter like you're banging a tambourine. Watch as the sugar falls through the sifter onto your baking like falling snow! Just like snow, this sugar doesn't last forever, so eat your dessert shortly after decorating!

# Cinnamon Sugar

To make about ½ cup of cinnamon sugar, use a mixing spoon to MIX 1 tablespoon of cinnamon into ½ cup of white sugar. Then start sprinkling!

# MILKS

Every dessert needs something creamy and refreshing to wash it down with. Take a slip on our milk straw slides. Here you'll find five superb recipes to slurp up! Race you to the bottom!

# Slam Dunk Vanilla Milk (GF)

### Makes ½ cup of syrup (enough for 8 glasses of milk)

Could there be a more perfect drink for dunking your cookies in? We don't think so!
Refreshing and sweet, this Slam Dunk Vanilla Milk goes with all desserts. A winner!

 Get Ready...

## TOOLS

- ☐ Measuring cups and spoons
- ☐ Medium saucepan
- ☐ Mixing spoon
- ☐ Oven mitts
- ☐ Small heatproof bowl
- ☐ Blender or a large jam jar with a tight-fitting lid

**There's more to explore!**
Go to the **Information Booth** on page 7 to discover more about boiling points.

## INGREDIENTS

| Vanilla Syrup | |
|---|---|
| 1 cup | white sugar |
| ½ cup | water |
| 1 teaspoon | vanilla extract |
| Slam Dunk Vanilla Milk | |
| 1 cup | whole milk |
| 1 teaspoon | milk powder |
| 1 tablespoon | Vanilla Syrup (recipe above) |

# . . . BAKE!

 Made on the stove, this recipe needs YOUR PERSON with you the whole time.

## Vanilla Syrup

1. To the saucepan, add the white sugar, water and vanilla extract. Set the saucepan on your stove. Turn the stove to medium heat and bring the mixture to a simmering boil.

2. Using the mixing spoon, MIX until the sugar has disappeared. Using the oven mitts, carefully remove the saucepan from the heat.

3. Pour the vanilla syrup into the heatproof bowl. Let cool to room temperature.

## Slam Dunk Vanilla Milk

1. Once the syrup has cooled, add the milk, instant milk powder and 1 tablespoon of the vanilla syrup to a blender or a large jam jar with a tight-fitting lid. Attach the lid and blend or shake for 30 seconds.

2. Pour the sweet, tasty milk into a glass. Score!

   **Save for later?** This milk should be enjoyed right away, but you can store the syrup in the fridge in an airtight container for up to 6 weeks.

Continue your baking adventure in **Cookieland** (page 37)! There you can try making a batch of cookies to dunk in your glass of milk! Our favorite flavor match is **7th Street Chocolate Chip Cookies** (page 39).

# Moo-vellous Strawberry Milk (GF)

### Makes ½ cup of syrup (enough for 5 glasses of milk)

Does strawberry milk come from a pink cow? Perhaps . . . but this
perfectly pink drink can be made right at home. How moo-vellous!

 Get Ready . . .

| TOOLS |
| --- |
| ☐ Measuring cups and spoons |
| ☐ Medium saucepan |
| ☐ Mixing spoon |
| ☐ Sifter |
| ☐ Small heatproof bowl |
| ☐ Oven mitts |
| ☐ Blender or a large jam jar with a tight-fitting lid |

| INGREDIENTS | |
| --- | --- |
| **Strawberry Syrup** | |
| 2 cups | frozen strawberries |
| ⅓ cup | white sugar |
| ¼ cup | water |
| ⅛ teaspoon | table salt |
| **Moo-vellous Strawberry Milk** | |
| 1 cup | whole milk or your favorite dairy-free milk |
| 1½ tablespoons | Strawberry Syrup (recipe above) |

**There's more to explore!**
Go to the **Information Booth** on page 7 to
discover more about boiling points.

# . . . BAKE!

 Made on the stove, this recipe needs YOUR PERSON with you the whole time.

## Strawberry Syrup

1. To the medium saucepan, add the strawberries, white sugar, water and salt. Place the saucepan on your stove. Turn the stove to medium heat and bring the mixture to a simmering boil.

 2. Once it's boiling, turn the heat down to medium-low. Continue to simmer for 10 minutes. Using the mixing spoon, MIX often.

3. Place the sifter over the small heatproof bowl. Using the oven mitts, carefully remove the saucepan from the heat.

4. Slowly and carefully pour the strawberry sauce into the sifter to separate the seeds from the syrup. The syrup will drain into the bowl below and the seeds will be left behind. Let the syrup cool completely at room temperature.

## Moo-vellous Strawberry Milk

1. Once the syrup has cooled, add the milk and 1½ tablespoons of the strawberry syrup to a blender or large jam jar with a tight-fitting lid. Attach the lid and blend or shake for 30 seconds.

2. Pour the perfectly pink strawberry milk into a glass. Enjoy!

**Save for later?** This milk should be enjoyed right away, but you can store the syrup in the fridge in an airtight container for up to 2 weeks.

**Continue your baking adventure** in **Cookieland** (page 37)! There you can try baking yummy cookies to go with your glass of milk! Our favorite flavor match is **Wonderland Cookies** (page 41)!

**And get creative!** To create the fancy decorations you see on the rims of the glasses in the photo opposite, you just need some melted chocolate and sprinkles. In a small heatproof bowl, melt a handful of chocolate melting wafers (they come in different colors!) in the microwave. Dip the rim of your empty glass into the melted chocolate. Pull the glass out and wait 5 seconds for the chocolate to begin to harden. Now dip the chocolate-coated rim into a bowl of your favorite sprinkles. Allow the rim to dry completely before filling the glass with your yummy milk!

Moo-vellous
Strawberry
Milk
(page 143)

Slam Dunk Vanilla Milk
(page 141)

Chocolate Milk Mustache
(page 146)

# Chocolate Milk Mustache (GF)

### Makes 2 cups of syrup (enough for 6 glasses of milk)

This milk is udderly awesome! It's rich and creamy and oh-so-chocolatey from its
two types of chocolate chips. Blowing bubbles and getting a milk mustache are both a MUST.

 Get Ready...

| TOOLS |
|---|
| ☐ Measuring cups and spoons |
| ☐ Medium saucepan |
| ☐ Mixing spoon |
| ☐ Oven mitts |
| ☐ Sifter |
| ☐ Small heatproof bowl |
| ☐ Blender or a large jam jar with a tight-fitting lid |

**There's more to explore!**
Go to the *Information Booth* on page 7 to
discover more about boiling points and room
temperature.

| INGREDIENTS | |
|---|---|
| **Chocolate Syrup** | |
| 1 cup | milk chocolate chips |
| ½ cup | white chocolate chips |
| 1 cup | whole milk |
| 2 teaspoons | vanilla extract |
| ¼ teaspoon | table salt |
| **Chocolate Milk Mustache** | |
| 1 cup | whole milk |
| ½ teaspoon | milk powder |
| ⅓ cup | Chocolate Syrup (recipe above) |

# . . . BAKE!

 Made on the stove, this recipe needs YOUR PERSON with you the whole time.

## Chocolate Syrup

1. To the saucepan, add the milk chocolate chips, white chocolate chips and whole milk. Place the saucepan on the stove. Turn the stove to medium-low heat and bring to a simmer.

2. Using the mixing spoon, MIX until all the chocolate has melted. Add the vanilla extract and salt. MIX for 1 more minute until everything is combined.

3. Using the oven mitts, carefully remove the saucepan from the heat.

4. Place the sifter on top of the small heatproof bowl. Carefully pour the chocolate syrup through the sifter to remove any lumps and let the syrup cool to room temperature on the counter.

## Chocolate Milk

1. Once the syrup has cooled, add the whole milk, milk powder and ⅓ cup of the chocolate syrup to a blender or large jam jar with a tight-fitting lid. Attach the lid and blend or shake for 30 seconds.

2. Pour the chocolate milk into a glass.

   **Save for later?** This milk should be enjoyed right away, but you can store the syrup in an airtight container in the fridge for up to 3 weeks.

 Continue your baking adventure in **Donutland** (page 153) and in **Wonderpark** at the **Toppings** (page 128)! There you can try baking up a batch of delish donuts to go with your milk! Our favorite flavor match is **Chocolate Date Donuts** (page 161) topped with **Chocolate Potato Chips** (page 133).

# Hot Cocoa (GF)

## Makes 2 mugs of cocoa (photo on page 49)

Warm up your belly with a yummy cup of cocoa! This easy-peasy recipe is our go-to drink on a cold day. Be sure to top it with Cloud Cream, Chocolate Bar Curls, Cinnamon Sugar . . . THE SKY'S THE LIMIT!

 Get Ready...

| TOOLS |
| --- |
| ☐ Measuring cups and spoons |
| ☐ Large (4-cup) spouted measuring cup |
| ☐ Whisk |
| ☐ Medium saucepan |
| ☐ Oven mitts |

| INGREDIENTS | |
| --- | --- |
| 2 teaspoons | cocoa powder |
| 4 teaspoons | white sugar |
| 2 cups | whole milk |
| 1 teaspoon | vanilla extract |

**There's more to explore!**
Go to the *Information Booth* on page 7 to discover more about boiling points.

**FUN FACT:** Did you know hot cocoa has been around since the time of the Ancient Mayans? It's a wonder it's not gotten cold . . .

# . . . BAKE!

 Made on the stove, this recipe needs YOUR PERSON with you the whole time.

 1. To the spouted measuring cup, add the cocoa powder and white sugar. Using the whisk, WHISK until everything is combined.

2. To the saucepan, add the milk and vanilla extract. Place the saucepan on your stove. Turn the stove to low heat and bring the milk to a simmer.

3. Using the oven mitts, slowly and carefully pour about ¼ cup of the hot milk into the spouted measuring cup with the cocoa powder mixture.

 4. WHISK until the mixture forms a paste.

5. Slowly and carefully pour the remaining hot milk into the cocoa mixture.

 6. WHISK gently until everything is combined.

7. Carefully pour the hot cocoa into 2 mugs and top with your favorite toppings!

Save for later? This hot cocoa should be enjoyed right away. Bottoms up!

 Continue your baking adventure in Wonderpark at the Toppings (page 128). There you can try making some terrific toppings for your hot cocoa! Our favorite flavor matches are Cloud Cream (page 129) and Chocolate Bar Curls (page 138)! Why stop there? Head to Cookieland (page 37) and bake a cookie to eat with your mug of cocoa. Our favorite flavor match is Poop Cookies (page 47).

# Polar Bear Hot Chocolate (GF)

Makes 1 cup of syrup (enough for 8 mugs of hot chocolate)
(photo on page 49)

This creamy mug of white hot chocolate is the perfect thing to sip on a snowy day!
Polar bear–approved!

 Get Ready...

| TOOLS |
| --- |
| ☐ Measuring cups and spoons |
| ☐ 2 medium saucepans |
| ☐ Oven mitts |
| ☐ Small spoon |
| ☐ Sifter |
| ☐ Small heatproof bowl |

| INGREDIENTS | |
| --- | --- |
| **White Chocolate Syrup** | |
| ½ cup | whipping cream |
| 1 cup | white chocolate chips |
| 2 teaspoons | salted butter |
| **Polar Bear Hot Chocolate** | |
| 1 cup | whole milk |
| 2 tablespoons | White Chocolate Syrup (recipe above) |

**There's more to explore!**
Go to the *Information Booth* on page 7 to discover more about boiling points.

# . . . BAKE!

 Made on the stove, this recipe needs YOUR PERSON with you the whole time.

## White Chocolate Syrup

1. To 1 saucepan, add the whipping cream. Place the saucepan on the stove. Turn the stove to medium-low heat and bring the cream to a simmer. Using the oven mitts, carefully remove the saucepan from the heat.

 2. Using the mixing spoon, MIX in the chocolate chips and butter until they're melted.

3. Place the sifter on top of the small heatproof bowl. Slowly and carefully pour the white chocolate syrup through the sifter to remove any lumps and let the syrup cool to room temperature on the counter.

## Polar Bear Hot Chocolate

1. To the other saucepan, add the milk. Place the saucepan on your stove. Turn the stove to medium-low heat and bring the milk to a simmer.

2. Using the oven mitts, carefully remove the saucepan from the heat.

3. Add 2 tablespoons of white chocolate syrup to a mug. Slowly and carefully pour the hot milk into your mug. Using the small spoon, stir until everything is blended.

   **Save for later?** This hot chocolate should be enjoyed right away, but you can store the syrup in an airtight container in the fridge for up to 7 days.

Continue your baking adventure in **Cookieland** (page 37)! There you can try making a batch of cookies to eat with your steamy drink! Our favorite flavor match is **Poop Cookies** (page 47)!

# Chapter 4

# DONUTLAND

Rev your engines, racers! Welcome to the donut speedway! Here you'll find six awesome recipes for baked donuts. Baked donuts are a great alternative to fried donuts because they're safer to make—and they're just as delicious to eat! On your mark, get set, GO!

# Shoe-nuts

### Makes 18 donuts

Roll into the kitchen to bake these yummy donuts! They are our fun take on a French cruller (a soft, airy donut with a crispy outside). Made like choux (which sounds like "shoe") pastry, the batter begins on the stove, so make sure YOUR PERSON is nearby to help you out. Weeeeee!

 Get Ready...

| TOOLS |
|---|
| ☐ Measuring cups and spoons |
| ☐ Medium saucepan |
| ☐ Mixing spoon |
| ☐ Oven mitts |
| ☐ Large bowl |
| ☐ Pastry brush |
| ☐ 3 donut pans (or 1 donut pan, used 3 times) |
| ☐ Big spoon |
| ☐ Large piping bag |
| ☐ Coupler and large star piping tip |
| ☐ Cooling racks |
| ☐ Butter knife |

| INGREDIENTS | |
|---|---|
| 1 cup | water |
| ½ cup | salted butter |
| 2 tablespoons | white sugar |
| 1 cup | all-purpose flour |
| Coconut oil, for greasing pans | |
| Cooking spray, for greasing pans | |
| 4 | large eggs, lightly beaten |

**There's more to explore!**
Go to the *Information Booth* on page 7 to discover more about piping and preparing your pans.

# . . . BAKE!

 1. FIND YOUR PERSON To the medium saucepan, add the water, butter and white sugar. Place the saucepan on your stove. Turn the stove to medium-high heat and bring the mixture to a boil. Once it's boiling, turn the heat down to low and add the flour.

 2. Using the mixing spoon, MIX slowly for 30 seconds. The batter should turn clumpy. Once it's clumpy, start stirring quickly until the dough forms into a ball, about 30 seconds.

 3. FIND YOUR PERSON Using the oven mitts, carefully remove the saucepan from the heat. Dump the dough ball into the large bowl and let it cool for 10 minutes.

4. Preheat your oven to 400°F. Dip the pastry brush into the coconut oil and brush the donut pans with it. Make sure you grease up the sides of each ring as well as the tops of the pans! Now lightly spray the pans with cooking spray.

 5. After the dough has cooled for 10 minutes, add the beaten eggs to the bowl with the dough. Using the mixing spoon, MIX the eggs into the dough. At first the batter will look really wet and lumpy. Keep stirring! Within 2 or 3 minutes the eggs will mix in and you'll have a thick, glossy batter. Don't give up!

6. Using the big spoon, scoop the shoe-nut batter into the large piping bag fitted with a coupler and large star piping tip.

7. Lightly squeeze a ring of shoe-nut batter into each ring of the donut pans to make 18 donuts.

 8. FIND YOUR PERSON Bake the shoe-nuts, 1 or 2 pans at a time, until golden brown, 18–20 minutes.

 9. FIND YOUR PERSON Using the oven mitts, carefully remove the donut pans from the oven and place them on the cooling racks. Let the shoe-nuts cool in the pans until they're cool enough to touch.

10. Once cool, run the tip of the butter knife between the edge of the pan and the donut to help get them out.

Save for later? These donuts are best enjoyed the day you make them but can be stored in an airtight container for up to 2 days (they will lose their crispiness).

 Continue your baking adventure in **Wonderpark** at the **Glazes and More** (page 116). There you can dip these donuts in one of our divine glazes! Our favorite flavor match is **The Bee's Knees Glaze** (page 123) or the **Chocolate Shine Glaze** (page 121)!

Shoe-nuts (page 154)
with Bee's Knee's Glaze
(page 123)

Shoe-nuts (page 154)
with Chocolate
Shine Glaze
(page 121)

# Pillow Donuts

### Makes about 16 donuts

If there were ever a dessert you could fall asleep on, our Pillow Donuts would be it! These baked yeast donuts are sooooo light and fluffy, they'll make you excited for bedtime! Ok . . . maybe *only* if one of these donuts is your bedtime snack. "I'm excited for bedtime," said NO KID EVER!

 Get Ready...

| TOOLS |
| --- |
| ☐ Measuring cups and spoons |
| ☐ 2 cookie sheets |
| ☐ Parchment paper or silicone baking mats |
| ☐ Medium saucepan |
| ☐ Oven mitts |
| ☐ 2 small bowls |
| ☐ 2 large bowls |
| ☐ Mixing spoon |
| ☐ Plastic wrap |
| ☐ 6–8-inch round cookie cutter |
| ☐ Cooling racks |

| INGREDIENTS | |
| --- | --- |
| 6 tablespoons | salted butter |
| 1¼ cups | whole milk, lukewarm |
| 2¼ teaspoons | quick active yeast |
| 4 cups | all-purpose flour + more for rolling and cutting |
| ¼ cup | white sugar |
| ½ teaspoon | sea salt |
| 3 | large eggs, lightly beaten |

**There's more to explore!**
Go to the **Information Booth** on page 7 to discover more about lukewarm temperature and kneading dough.

# . . . BAKE!

1. Line 2 cookie sheets with parchment paper or silicone baking mats. Set the cookie sheets to the side.

2. FIND YOUR PERSON Add the butter to the saucepan. Place the saucepan on the stove. Turn the stove to low heat and gently melt the butter. Using the oven mitts, carefully remove the saucepan from the heat. Let the butter cool for 5 minutes.

3. To the small bowl, add the lukewarm milk and yeast. Let it rest for 10 minutes.

4. To 1 large bowl, add the cooled melted butter, yeasty milk mixture (it should be kinda bubbly), 4 cups of flour, white sugar, salt and lightly beaten eggs. Using the mixing spoon and working very slowly, MIX everything together until the mixture begins to form a ball. The dough will be very sticky.

5. Sprinkle your countertop with some flour and dump the dough out onto the floured surface.

6. Using your HANDS, knead the dough for 10 minutes. If it begins to stick to your surface, sprinkle it with more flour.

7. After 10 minutes (we bet your hands are tired!), place the dough in the other large bowl. Cover the bowl with a sheet of plastic wrap. Leave the bowl on the countertop and let the dough rise until it has doubled in size, about 1½ hours.

. . .

8. Sprinkle your countertop with flour. Dump the risen dough onto the lightly floured surface. Using your HANDS, shape the dough into a long thin rectangle about ½-inch high (that's about the size of your thumbnail). Add more flour to your hands and work surface if anything starts to get sticky!

9. To the second small bowl, add a little flour. Dip the rim of the round cookie cutter into the flour. Now press the floured cookie cutter down into the dough and turn your hand like you're turning a doorknob. Yay! You just cut a circle! Repeat to cut as many circles as possible from the dough.

10. Now it's time to remove the dough circles. Start by peeling away the scraps of dough from around the circles. Mush these scraps back into a ball. Using your fingers and working with 1 circle at a time, peel the dough circles off your work surface and gently place them, evenly spaced, on 1 of the cookie sheets.

11. Repeat these steps with the remaining dough until you have about 8 evenly spaced donuts on each cookie sheet. Let the donuts sit out on the cookie sheets for 30 minutes to rise again.

12. Preheat your oven to 375°F.

*Recipe continues*

**13.** FIND YOUR PERSON Bake the donuts, 1 cookie sheet at a time, until golden brown, about 10–12 minutes.

 **14.** FIND YOUR PERSON Using the oven mitts, carefully remove the cookie sheets from the oven and place them on the cooling racks. Let the donuts cool completely on the cookie sheets.

**Save for later?** These donuts are best enjoyed the day you make them but can be stored in an airtight container for up to 2 days.

Continue your baking adventure in **Wonderpark** at the **Fillings** (page 84). There you can try filling this donut with one of our yummy fillings! Our favorite flavor match for these donuts is the **Jam Out Berry Jam!** (page 96). Then head to **Toppings** and dust them in **Sugar Snow** (page 139)!

Sugar Snow
(page 139)

Jam Out
Berry Jam
(page 96)

# Chocolate Date Donuts

## Makes 12 donuts

Make a date with these gluten-free, vegan treats! These fudgy and perfectly
sweet donuts are made with dates and they are DELICIOUS!
This recipe requires a little extra mixing muscle so a food processor is a MUST!

## TOOLS

- ☐ Measuring cups and spoons
- ☐ Pastry brush
- ☐ 2 donut pans (or 1 donut pan, used 2 times)
- ☐ Medium bowl
- ☐ Mixing spoon
- ☐ Food processor fitted with the S blade
- ☐ Spatula
- ☐ Electric mixer
- ☐ Big spoon
- ☐ Large piping bag
- ☐ Coupler and large round piping tip
- ☐ Oven mitts
- ☐ Toothpicks
- ☐ Cooling racks
- ☐ Butter knife

## INGREDIENTS

| | |
|---|---|
| Coconut oil, for greasing pans | |
| Cooking spray, for greasing pans | |
| 1 cup | gluten-free 1:1 baking flour |
| ½ cup | cocoa powder |
| ⅛ teaspoon | table salt |
| 1 cup | pitted Medjool dates, chopped |
| ½ cup | light brown sugar |
| 1 cup | almond milk |
| ¼ cup | almond butter |
| 1 teaspoon | vanilla extract |
| 2 teaspoons | baking powder |
| ½ teaspoon | baking soda |

### There's more to explore!

Go to the **Information Booth** on page 7 to discover more about piping and preparing your pans.

# . . . BAKE!

1. Preheat your oven to 350°F. Dip the pastry brush into the coconut oil and brush the insides of the donut pans with oil, making sure to grease up the sides as well as the top! Now lightly spray the pans with cooking spray.

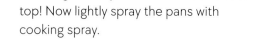

2. To the medium bowl, add the gluten-free flour, cocoa powder and salt. Using the mixing spoon, MIX until the mixture is lump-free. Set this bowl to the side.

3. To the bowl of the food processor, add the chopped dates, light brown sugar, almond milk, almond butter and vanilla extract.

4. FIND YOUR PERSON Turn the food processor on at high speed. Blend until the mixture looks like mush, about 1 minute. Add the baking powder and baking soda to the food processor. Blend for another 30 seconds.

5. Pour the date mixture into the bowl with the flour mixture. Using the spatula, SCRAPE down the sides and bottom of the bowl of the food processor.

6. Using the electric mixer, BEAT on medium-low speed until everything is mixed together.

7. Using the big spoon, scoop the donut batter into the large piping bag with a coupler and large round piping tip attached. Squeeze a ring of donut batter into each ring of the donut pans to make 12 donuts.

8. FIND YOUR PERSON Bake the donuts, 1 or 2 pans at a time, until a toothpick stuck into a donut comes out clean, about 10–12 minutes.

9. FIND YOUR PERSON Using the oven mitts, carefully remove the donut pans from the oven and place them on the cooling racks. Let the donuts cool completely in the pans.

10. Once cool, run the tip of the butter knife between the edge of the pans and the donuts to help get them out.

**Save for later?** These donuts are best enjoyed the day you make them but can be stored in an airtight container for up to 2 days.

**Continue your baking adventure** in **Wonderpark** at the **Glazes and More** (page 116) for some gla-mazing recipes! We like to glaze these donuts with **It's Good, Eh? Glaze** (page 117) and then drizzle with different colors of **Her Royal Highness Icing** (page 118)! Then top with some cool sprinkles! Looking for even more chocolate? Try dunking one of these donuts in a delicious glass of **Chocolate Milk Mustache** (page 146).

It's Good, Eh?
Glaze
(page 117)

Stuff
(page 138)

Her Royal
Highness Icing
(page 118)

# I'm Coconuts for You! Donuts ⓖⓕ

### Makes 18 donuts

Like the name suggests, we're nutty for these coconut donuts! We dare you to make them more bonkers by topping them with our Toasted Coconut (page 132). This batter loves to stick to the donut pans, so be sure to grease your wheels heavily! (Discover more on page 16.)

 Get Ready. . .

## TOOLS

- ☐ Measuring cups and spoons
- ☐ Pastry brush
- ☐ 3 donut pans (or 1 donut pan, used 3 times)
- ☐ Small bowl
- ☐ Mixing spoon
- ☐ Small saucepan
- ☐ Oven mitts
- ☐ Large bowl
- ☐ Spatula
- ☐ Electric mixer
- ☐ Big spoon
- ☐ Spouted measuring cup
- ☐ Toothpicks
- ☐ Butter knife
- ☐ Cooling racks

**There's more to explore!**
Go to the **Information Booth** on page 7 to discover more about preparing your pans.

## INGREDIENTS

| | |
|---|---|
| ¼ cup | coconut oil + extra for greasing pans |
| Cooking spray, for greasing pans | |
| 1¾ cups | gluten-free 1:1 baking flour |
| ½ cup | sweetened coconut flakes |
| ¼ teaspoon | table salt |
| ¼ cup | salted butter |
| ½ cup | light brown sugar |
| ½ cup | white sugar |
| 2 | large eggs |
| 2 teaspoons | baking powder |
| ¼ teaspoon | baking soda |
| ½ cup | whole milk |
| ¼ cup | applesauce |
| 1 teaspoon | vanilla extract |

# . . . BAKE!

1. Preheat your oven to 350°F.

2. Dip the pastry brush into the coconut oil and brush the insides of the donut pans with it, making sure to grease up the sides as well as the top! Now lightly spray the pans with cooking spray.

3. To the small bowl, add the gluten-free flour, coconut flakes and salt. Using the mixing spoon, MIX until everything is combined. Set this bowl to the side.

4. FIND YOUR PERSON To the small saucepan, add the ¼ cup coconut oil and the butter. Place the saucepan on your stove. Turn the stove to low heat and gently melt the butter. Using the oven mitts, carefully remove the saucepan from the heat.

5. Pour the butter mixture into the large bowl. Using the spatula, SCRAPE down the sides and bottom of the saucepan, adding every last drop to the bowl.

6. Add the light brown sugar and white sugar to the bowl with the butter mixture. Using the electric mixer, BEAT on medium speed for 1 minute. Add the eggs. BEAT on medium speed until everything is combined. Add the baking powder, baking soda, milk, applesauce and vanilla extract. BEAT on medium speed until everything is mixed together.

7. Add the flour mixture to the bowl with the butter and sugar mixture. BEAT on low speed until everything is combined.

8. Using the spatula, SCRAPE down the sides and bottom of the bowl.

9. BEAT on medium speed for 20 seconds. The batter should be very wet. Let the donut batter rest for 10 minutes.

10. Using the big spoon, scoop the donut batter into the spouted measuring cup. Pour a layer of batter around each donut ring, filling each ring ⅔ of the way up.

11. FIND YOUR PERSON Bake the donuts, 1 or 2 pans at a time, until a toothpick stuck into a donut comes out clean, about 10–12 minutes.

12. FIND YOUR PERSON Using the oven mitts, carefully remove the donut pans from the oven and place them on the cooling racks. Let the donuts cool completely in their pans.

13. Once cool, run the tip of the butter knife between the edge of the pans and the donuts to help get them out.

Save for later? These donuts are best enjoyed the day you make them but can be stored in an airtight container for up to 2 days.

Continue your baking adventure in **Wonderpark** at the **Glazes and More** (page 116) and **Toppings** (page 128)! There you can try glazing this donut AND topping it with one of our superb toppings! Our favorite flavor match is **It's Good, Eh? Glaze** (page 117) and **Toasted Coconut** (page 132)!

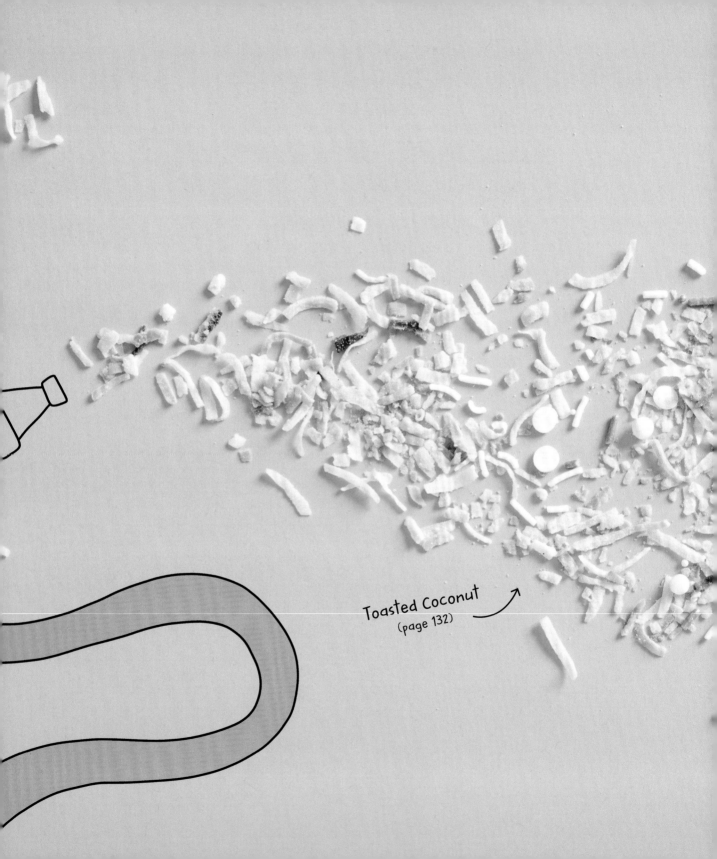

Toasted Coconut
(page 132)

Stuff
(page 138)

I'm Coconuts
for You
(page 164)

Cinnamon Sugar
(page 139)

It's Good, Eh? Glaze
(page 117)

# Sugar and Spice and Everything Nice Donuts

## Makes 18 donuts

These lil' donuts make us smile! They're made with sugar and spice and everything nice!

 Get Ready...

## TOOLS

- ☐ Measuring cups and spoons
- ☐ Pastry brush
- ☐ 3 donut pans (or 1 donut pan, used 3 times)
- ☐ Medium saucepan
- ☐ Oven mitts
- ☐ Large bowl
- ☐ Whisk
- ☐ Small bowl
- ☐ Mixing spoon
- ☐ Big spoon
- ☐ Large piping bag
- ☐ Coupler and large round piping tip
- ☐ Toothpicks
- ☐ Butter knife
- ☐ Cooling racks

## INGREDIENTS

| | |
|---|---|
| Coconut oil, for greasing pans | |
| Cooking spray, for greasing pans | |
| ¼ cup | salted butter |
| 2 cups | all-purpose flour |
| ⅓ cup | superfine sugar |
| 2 tablespoons | milk powder |
| 1½ teaspoons | baking powder |
| ½ teaspoon | baking soda |
| ½ teaspoon | ground nutmeg |
| ¼ teaspoon | ground cinnamon |
| ¼ teaspoon | ground ginger |
| ⅛ teaspoon | table salt |
| 1 cup | buttermilk |
| 2 | large eggs |
| 1 tablespoon | vegetable oil |
| 1 teaspoon | vanilla extract |

**There's more to explore!**
Go to the **Information Booth** on page 7 to discover more about preparing your pans.

# . . . BAKE!

1. Preheat your oven to 350°F. Dip the pastry brush into the coconut oil and brush the insides of the donut pans with oil, making sure to grease up the sides as well as the top! Now lightly spray the pans with cooking spray.

 2. FIND YOUR PERSON To the saucepan, add the butter. Place the saucepan on the stove. Turn the stove to low heat and gently melt the butter. Using the oven mitts, carefully remove the saucepan from the heat. Let the butter cool for 5 minutes.

 3. To the large bowl, add the flour, sugar, milk powder, baking powder, baking soda, ground nutmeg, ground cinnamon, ground ginger and salt. Using the whisk, WHISK until the mixture is lump-free. Set this bowl to the side.

 4. To the small bowl, add the cooled melted butter, buttermilk, eggs, vegetable oil and vanilla extract. WHISK until everything is combined.

 5. Slowly add the buttermilk mixture to the large bowl with the flour mixture. Using the mixing spoon, MIX until everything is combined. It's ok if the batter is a little lumpy.

6. Using the big spoon, scoop the donut batter into the large piping bag fitted with a coupler and large round piping tip. Squeeze a ring of donut batter into each ring of the donut pans.

 7. FIND YOUR PERSON Bake the donuts, 1 or 2 pans at a time, until a toothpick stuck into a donut comes out clean, about 10–12 minutes.

 8. FIND YOUR PERSON Using the oven mitts, carefully remove the donut pans from the oven and place them on the cooling racks. Let the donuts cool completely in their pans.

9. Once cool, run the tip of the butter knife between the edge of the pans and the donuts to help get them out.

**Save for later?** These donuts are best enjoyed the day you make them but can be stored in an airtight container for up to 2 days.

 Continue your baking adventure in **Wonderpark** at the **Glazes and More** (page 116) for some gla-mazing recipes! There you can try making a glaze to coat these donuts with. Our favorite flavor match is **It's Good, Eh? Glaze** (page 117). Then head to **Toppings** (page 128) and top them with **Cinnamon Sugar** (page 139) and a sprinkling of star-shaped sprinkles.

# Baked Strawberries and Cream Donuts

## Makes 18 donuts

Made with strawberries baked in maple syrup and rich sour cream, these donuts
are a delight to make and even more delightful to eat!

 Get Ready...

## TOOLS

- ☐ Measuring cups and spoons
- ☐ Cookie sheet
- ☐ Parchment paper or a silicone baking mat
- ☐ Medium bowl
- ☐ Mixing spoon
- ☐ Oven mitts
- ☐ Cooling racks
- ☐ Butter knife
- ☐ Small bowl
- ☐ Whisk
- ☐ Large bowl
- ☐ Electric mixer
- ☐ Spatula
- ☐ Pastry brush
- ☐ 3 donut pans (or 1 donut pan, used 3 times)
- ☐ Big spoon
- ☐ Large piping bag
- ☐ Coupler and large round piping tip
- ☐ Toothpicks

### There's more to explore!

Go to the **Information Booth** on page 7 to
discover more about piping and preparing
your pans.

## INGREDIENTS

| Baked Strawberries | |
|---|---|
| 2 cups | sliced strawberries |
| 1 tablespoon | pure maple syrup |
| ¼ teaspoon | ground cinnamon |

| Donuts | |
|---|---|
| 2 cups | all-purpose flour |
| 2 teaspoons | baking powder |
| ½ teaspoon | baking soda |
| ½ teaspoon | table salt |
| ¼ teaspoon | ground cinnamon |
| ½ cup | salted butter |
| ½ cup | light brown sugar |
| ¼ cup | white sugar |
| 3 | large eggs |
| 1 cup | sour cream |
| 2 teaspoons | vanilla extract |
| Coconut oil, for greasing pans | |
| Cooking spray, for greasing pans | |

# . . . BAKE!

## Baked Strawberries

1. Preheat your oven to 350°F. Line the cookie sheet with parchment paper or a silicone baking mat.

2. To the medium bowl, add the strawberries, maple syrup and ground cinnamon. Using the mixing spoon, MIX until everything is coated in maple syrup.

3. Spoon the strawberry mixture onto the cookie sheet. Spread the strawberries out evenly.

4. FIND YOUR PERSON Bake the strawberries in your oven for 18 minutes until they have shrunk in size and turned a deep red color.

5. FIND YOUR PERSON Using the oven mitts, carefully remove the cookie sheet from your oven and place it on a cooling rack. Let the strawberries cool completely on the cookie sheet.

6. Using the butter knife, cut the strawberries into tiny pieces, as big as a pea. Set the strawberries to the side.

## Donuts

7. To the small bowl, add the flour, baking powder, baking soda, salt and cinnamon. Using the whisk, WHISK until the mixture is lump-free. Set this bowl to the side.

8. To the large bowl, add the butter, light brown sugar and white sugar. Using the electric mixer, BEAT on medium speed until the mixture is light and fluffy, about 2 minutes. Add the eggs, sour cream and vanilla extract. BEAT on medium speed until everything is combined.

9. Using the spatula, SCRAPE down the sides and bottom of the bowl.

10. Add the flour mixture to the bowl with the butter and sugar mixture. BEAT on low speed until everything is combined.

11. Using the mixing spoon, MIX in the baked strawberries.

12. Dip the pastry brush into the coconut oil and brush the insides of the donut pans with oil, making sure to grease up the sides as well as the top! Lightly spray the donut pans with cooking spray.

13. Using the big spoon, scoop the donut batter into the large piping bag fitted with a coupler and large round piping tip. Squeeze a ring of donut batter into each mold of the donut pans.

14. FIND YOUR PERSON Bake the donuts, 1 or 2 pans at a time, until a toothpick stuck into a donut comes out clean, about 14–16 minutes.

15. FIND YOUR PERSON Using the oven mitts, carefully remove the donut pans from the oven and place them on the cooling racks. Let the donuts cool completely in the pans.

16. Once cool, run the tip of the butter knife between the edge of the pans and the donuts to help them get out.

   Save for later? These donuts are best enjoyed the day you make them but can be stored in an airtight container for up to 2 days.

   Continue your baking adventure in **Wonderpark** at the **Glazes and More** (page 116)! There you can try glazing this stellar strawberry donut with one of our gaga-good glazes! Our favorite flavor match is **Her Royal Highness Icing** (page 118), tinted bright pink and topped with sprinkles.

Chapter 5

# CAKELAND

Imagine floors made of chocolate crumbs and walls of layered lemon cake . . . Welcome to the cake castle! The sweetest place you'll ever visit! Here you'll find six of our greatest cake recipes ready for you to bake, fill and decorate. Now be our guest and enjoy your stay!

Stuff
(page 138)

Strawberry
Patch Frosting
(page 114)

Jam Out Berry Jam
(page 96)

# Pink Cake

## Makes 1 × 2-tiered cake

We're sweet on this cake's natural pink coloring made from a zippy strawberry puree!
You can make it even pinker by adding food coloring to the batter. Yay, pink!

 Get Ready...

| TOOLS |
|-------|
| ☐ Measuring cups and spoons |
| ☐ Medium saucepan |
| ☐ Mixing spoon |
| ☐ Oven mitts |
| ☐ Blender |
| ☐ Sifter |
| ☐ Small bowl |
| ☐ 2 × 8-inch cake pans |
| ☐ Parchment paper |
| ☐ 3 large bowls |
| ☐ Whisk |
| ☐ Toothpicks |
| ☐ Cooling racks |

| INGREDIENTS | |
|---|---|
| **Strawberry Puree** | |
| 4½ cups | frozen strawberries, thawed |
| **Cake** | |
| Cooking spray, for greasing pans | |
| 2¼ cups | all-purpose flour |
| 1½ teaspoons | baking soda |
| 1 teaspoon | table salt |
| 1½ cups | white sugar |
| 3 | whole eggs |
| ⅔ cup | vegetable oil |
| ½ cup | buttermilk |
| 1 teaspoon | vanilla extract |
| 1–2 teaspoons | red food coloring, optional |

**There's more to explore!**
Go to the **Information Booth** on page 7 to discover more about preparing your pans.

# . . . BAKE!

## Strawberry Puree

1. FIND YOUR PERSON To the saucepan, add the thawed strawberries and their juice. Place the saucepan on your stove. Turn the stove to medium heat and bring the strawberries to a boil. Turn down the heat to medium-low and cook for 15 minutes.

2. Using the mixing spoon, MIX the strawberries every 5 minutes.

3. FIND YOUR PERSON Using the oven mitts, carefully remove the saucepan from the heat. Let the strawberries cool to room temperature.

4. FIND YOUR PERSON Pour the cooled strawberries into the blender and blend for 30 seconds until soupy.

5. Place the sifter on top of the small bowl and pour the strawberry puree through it. This will catch all the strawberry seeds. You may need to use the mixing spoon to help push the puree through. Set the puree to the side.

## Cake

1. Preheat your oven to 350°F. Line the bottom of both cake pans with parchment paper circles. Spray the parchment paper and sides of the pans with cooking spray.

2. To 1 large bowl, add the flour, baking soda and salt. Using the whisk, WHISK until the mixture is lump-free. Set this bowl to the side.

3. To the other large bowl, add 1¼ cups of the the strawberry puree and the white sugar, eggs, vegetable oil, buttermilk, vanilla extract and food coloring, if using. WHISK until everything is combined.

4. Add the flour mixture to the large bowl with the strawberry mixture. WHISK until everything is combined.

5. Pour the batter evenly into the prepared pans.

6. FIND YOUR PERSON Bake both cakes until a toothpick stuck into the middle of each cake comes out clean, about 30–35 minutes.

7. FIND YOUR PERSON Using the oven mitts, carefully remove the cake pans from the oven and place them on the cooling racks. Let the cakes cool completely in the pans before removing them. Remember to remove the parchment paper if it's stuck to their bottoms!

**Save for later?** Store the cake in an airtight container for up to 2 days.

Continue your baking adventure in **Wonderpark** at the **Fillings** (page 84) and **Frostings** (page 102)! There you can try making one of our zingy fillings to fill this cake with AND one of our lip-smacking frostings! Our favorite flavor matches are **Jam Out Berry Jam!** for the filling (page 96) and **Strawberry Patch Frosting** (page 114). Decorate it with ALL THE PINK STUFF you can find (we used cotton candy and sprinkles)!

# Disappearing Chocolate Cake

### Makes 1 × 2-tiered cake

"Where did the cake go?" is what you'll be saying seconds after serving
this rich and irresistible chocolate cake. Chocolatey, moist and delicious,
it will be gone so fast, it'll be like it magically disappeared!

 Get Ready...

## TOOLS

☐ Measuring cups and spoons

☐ 2 × 8-inch round cake pans

☐ Parchment paper

☐ Large bowl

☐ Whisk

☐ Small bowl

☐ Spatula

☐ Electric mixer

☐ Toothpicks

☐ Oven mitts

☐ Cooling racks

## INGREDIENTS

| Cooking spray, for greasing pans | |
|---|---|
| 2 cups | all-purpose flour |
| 1½ cups | white sugar |
| ¾ cup | cocoa powder |
| 1 teaspoon | baking soda |
| 1 teaspoon | table salt |
| ½ cup | sour cream |
| ½ cup | vegetable oil |
| 1½ tablespoons | vanilla extract |
| 1½ cups | boiling water |

**There's more to explore!**
Go to the **Information Booth** on page 7 to
discover more about preparing your pans.

# . . . BAKE!

1. Preheat your oven to 350°F. Line the bottom of both cake pans with parchment paper circles. Spray the parchment paper and sides of the pans with cooking spray.

2. To the large bowl, add the flour, white sugar, cocoa powder, baking soda and salt. Using the whisk, WHISK until the mixture is lump-free. Set this bowl to the side.

3. To the small bowl, add the sour cream, vegetable oil and vanilla extract. WHISK until everything is combined.

4. Add the sour cream mixture to the large bowl with the flour mixture. Using the spatula, SCRAPE down the sides and bottom of the small bowl, adding every last drop to the large bowl.

5. Using the electric mixer, BEAT on low speed until everything is combined, about 1 minute.

6. FIND YOUR PERSON Slowly and carefully add the boiling water.

7. BEAT on low speed until the batter is shiny, about 2 minutes more.

8. Pour the batter evenly into the prepared cake pans. SCRAPE down the sides and bottom of the bowl, adding every last drop to the pans.

9. FIND YOUR PERSON Bake both cakes until a toothpick stuck into the middle of each cake comes out clean, about 20–24 minutes.

10. FIND YOUR PERSON Using the oven mitts, carefully remove the cake pans from the oven and place them on the cooling racks. Let the cakes cool completely in the pans before removing them. Remember to remove the parchment paper if it's stuck to their bottoms!

**Save for later?** Store the cake in an airtight container for up to 4 days.

Yolk yolk yolk! Which sweetie never arrives on time? Choco-late!

**Continue your baking adventure** in **Wonderpark** at the **Fillings** (page 84) and **Frostings** (page 102)! There you can try filling and frosting this cake with our fabulous fillings and fun frostings! Our favorite flavor matches are **Fudge! Filling** (page 92) and **Nutty Peanut Butter Frosting** (page 103)! And we love making **Chocolate Bar Curls** (page 138) to sprinkle on top.

Chocolate
Bar Curls
(page 138)

Nutty Peanut
Butter Frosting
(page 103)

Fudge! Filling
(page 92)

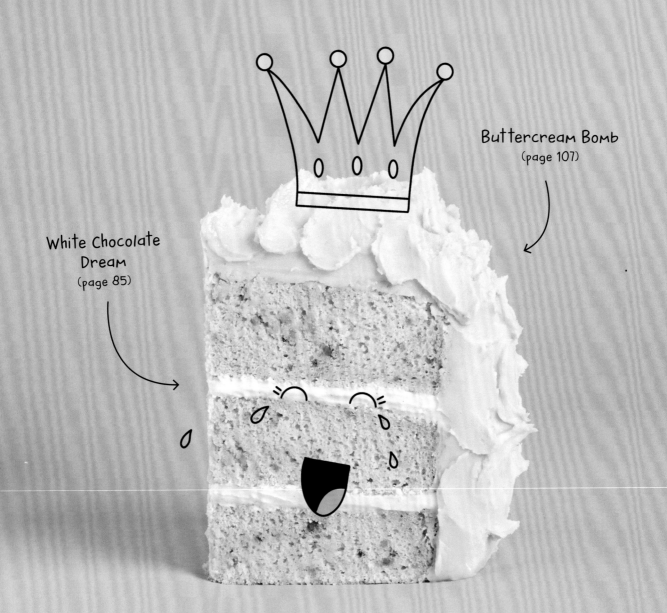

White Chocolate
Dream
(page 85)

Buttercream Bomb
(page 107)

# Confetti Cake (GF)

## Makes 1 × 9-inch cake

Have you ever been so happy you've cried? That's the way we feel when we make this cake!
It's delicious, gluten-free and so pretty—adding sprinkles to the batter makes you feel like
there's a rainbow in every bite! To make a 3-tiered cake like the picture opposite,
make three of these cakes for three times the fun!

 ☑ Get Ready...

| TOOLS |
|---|
| ☐ Measuring cups and spoons |
| ☐ 9-inch cake pan |
| ☐ Parchment paper |
| ☐ Medium saucepan |
| ☐ Oven mitts |
| ☐ Small bowl |
| ☐ Whisk |
| ☐ 2 large bowls |
| ☐ Electric mixer |
| ☐ Spatula |
| ☐ Toothpicks |
| ☐ Cooling rack |

### INGREDIENTS

| | |
|---|---|
| Cooking spray, for greasing the pan | |
| ½ cup | salted butter |
| 1½ cups | gluten-free 1:1 baking flour |
| ⅛ teaspoon | table salt |
| ¾ cup | white sugar |
| 2 teaspoons | baking powder |
| ¼ teaspoon | baking soda |
| 1 cup | whole milk, at room temperature |
| 1 teaspoon | vanilla extract |
| 6 | large egg whites |
| 2 tablespoons | rainbow sprinkles—we like to use round-shaped sprinkles |

**There's more to explore!**

Go to the **Information Booth** on page 7 to
discover more about separating eggs,
whipping peaks, room temperature and
preparing your pans.

# . . . BAKE!

1. Preheat your oven to 350°F. Line the bottom of the cake pan with a parchment paper circle. Spray the parchment paper and sides of the pan with cooking spray.

2. **FIND YOUR PERSON** To the saucepan, add the butter. Place the saucepan on your stove. Turn the stove to low heat and gently melt the butter. Using the oven mitts, carefully remove the saucepan from the heat. Let the butter cool for 5 minutes.

3. To the small bowl, add the flour and salt. Using the whisk, **WHISK** until the mixture is lump-free. Set this bowl to the side.

4. To 1 of the large bowls, add the egg whites. Using the electric mixer, **BEAT** the egg whites on high speed until stiff peaks form.

5. To the other large bowl, add the cooled melted butter and white sugar. Using the electric mixer, **BEAT** on medium-low speed until everything is combined. Add the baking powder, baking soda, milk and vanilla extract. **BEAT** on medium-low speed until everything is mixed together.

6. Add the flour mixture to the bowl with the butter and sugar mixture. **BEAT** on medium-low speed until combined.

7. Using the spatula, into the batter an

8. Now gently **FOLD** Be careful not to want the color to

9. Pour the batter .. **SCRAPE** down the sides and bottom of the bowl, getting every last drop in the pan.

10. **FIND YOUR PERSON** Bake the cake until a toothpick stuck into the middle of the cake comes out clean, about 38–40 minutes.

11. **FIND YOUR PERSON** Using the oven mitts, carefully remove the cake pan from the oven and place it on the cooling rack. Let the cake cool completely in the pan before removing it. Remember to remove the parchment paper if it's stuck to the bottom!

**Save for later?** Store the cake in an airtight container for up to 2 days.

> Continue your baking adventure in **Wonderpark** at the **Fillings** (page 84) and **Frostings** (page 102). Try one of our superb fillings and frostings to go with this cake! Our favorite flavor matches are **White Chocolate Dream** (page 85) for the filling and **Buttercream Bomb** (page 107) tinted turquoise for the frosting!

# Caramel Apple Cake Ⓥ

### Makes 1 × 2-tiered cake

We're *all over* this apple-filled vegan cake! Moist and full of fun texture, this cake is sure to be a hit. Be sure to make the Ooey Caramel (page 126) before you begin to make the cake! And if you'd like to decorate this cake just like a caramel apple you'd find at the fair (like we did for the photo on page 187), double the caramel recipe for double the fun!

 ☑ Get Ready...

## TOOLS

- ☐ Measuring cups and spoons
- ☐ 2 x 9-inch cake pans
- ☐ Parchment paper
- ☐ Large bowl
- ☐ Whisk
- ☐ 2 large bowls
- ☐ Spatula
- ☐ Oven mitts
- ☐ Toothpicks
- ☐ Cooling rack

🔍 **There's more to explore!**
Go to the **Information Booth** on page 7 to discover more about preparing your pans.

## INGREDIENTS

| | |
|---|---|
| 1 cup | Ooey Caramel Drizzle (page 126) |
| Cooking spray, for greasing pan | |
| 5 cups | cake and pastry flour |
| 2 cups | white sugar |
| 2 teaspoons | table salt |
| 2 teaspoons | ground cinnamon |
| 2 | medium apples, peeled, cored and grated |
| 2 cups | applesauce |
| 1 cup | vegetable oil |
| 1 cup | boiling water |
| 2 teaspoons | caramel extract |
| 2 teaspoons | baking soda |

# . . . BAKE!

1. Preheat your oven to 350°F. Cover the bottom of the cake pans with a parchment paper circles. Spray the parchment paper and sides of the pan with cooking spray.

2. To 1 large bowl, add the cake and pastry flour, white sugar, salt and ground cinnamon. Using the whisk, WHISK until the mixture is lump-free. Set this bowl to the side.

3. FIND YOUR PERSON To the other large bowl, add the grated apple, applesauce, vegetable oil, boiling water, caramel extract and baking soda.

4. WHISK until everything is combined.

5. Add the apple mixture to the flour mixture. WHISK until everything is combined.

6. Pour the batter evenly into the prepared cake pans. Using the spatula, SCRAPE down the sides and bottom of the bowl, getting every last drop into the pans.

7. Drizzle ½ cup of Ooey Caramel on top of the batter in each pan. Using the tip of the spatula, swirl the caramel into the batter.

8. FIND YOUR PERSON Bake both cakes, until a toothpick stuck into the middle of each cake comes out clean, 40–45 minutes.

9. FIND YOUR PERSON Using the oven mitts, carefully remove the cake pans from the oven and place them on the cooling rack. Let the cakes cool completely in the pans before removing them. Remember to remove the parchment paper circles if they're stuck to the bottoms!

**Save for later?** This cake is best enjoyed the day you make it but can be stored in an airtight container for up to 2 days.

**Continue your baking adventure** in **Wonderpark** at the **Frostings** (page 102)! There you can try filling this cake with one of our awesome frostings! Our favorite vegan flavor match is **Marvelous Mallow Frosting** (page 109). Then we drizzle or smear the cake with more **Ooey Caramel Drizzle** (page 126) and cover it with **Stuff** (page 138) like crushed peanuts.

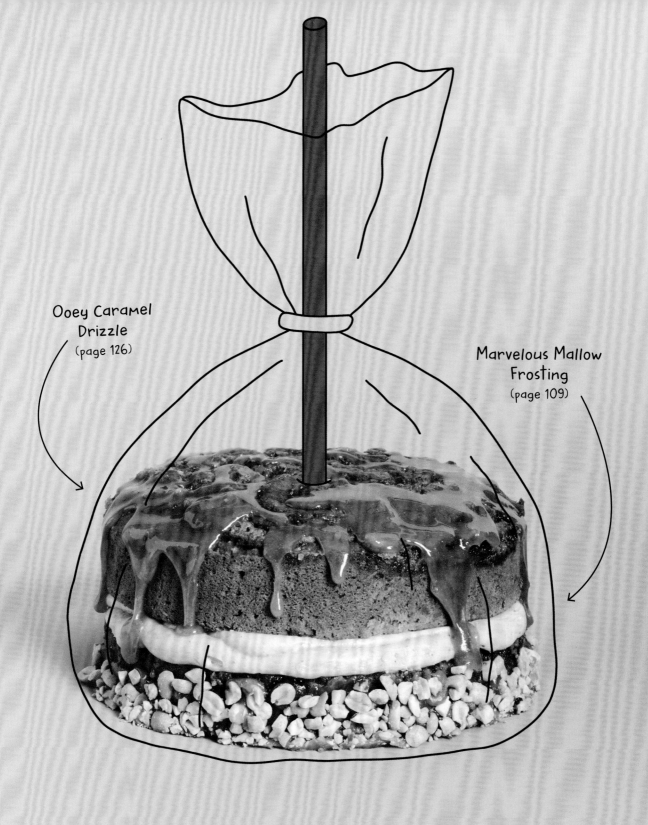

Ooey Caramel
Drizzle
(page 126)

Marvelous Mallow
Frosting
(page 109)

Chocolate Shine
Glaze
(page 121)

Chocolate Potato
Chips and Pretzels
(page 133)

# Chipper Chocolate Chip Cake

### Makes 1 round tube cake

No wonder this cake is so chipper. It looks like a giant donut, and it has three types of chocolate chips in it! Make it even more chip-tastic by decorating it with Chocolate Potato Chips and Pretzels (page 133)! It's super important to bake this fluffy cake in an ungreased tube pan, for the ultimate rise.

 Get Ready...

| TOOLS |
|---|
| ☐ Measuring cups and spoons |
| ☐ 2 large bowls |
| ☐ Electric mixer |
| ☐ Whisk |
| ☐ Big spoon |
| ☐ Spatula |
| ☐ Small bowl |
| ☐ Mixing spoon |
| ☐ Tube cake pan |
| ☐ Wooden skewer |
| ☐ Oven mitts |
| ☐ Cooling rack |

| INGREDIENTS | |
|---|---|
| 6 | large eggs, separated |
| ½ teaspoon | cream of tartar |
| 2¼ cups | cake and pastry flour |
| 1¾ cups | white sugar |
| 1 tablespoon | baking powder |
| 1 teaspoon | table salt |
| ¾ cup | cold water |
| ½ cup | vegetable oil |
| 2½ teaspoons | vanilla extract |
| ½ cup | mini semisweet chocolate chips |
| ½ cup | mini white chocolate chips |
| ½ cup | mini peanut butter chips |
| ½ teaspoon | all-purpose flour |

### There's more to explore!

Go to the **Information Booth** on page 7 to discover more about separating eggs and whipping peaks.

# . . . BAKE!

1. Preheat your oven to 325°F.

2. To 1 large bowl, add the egg whites and cream of tartar. Using the electric mixer, BEAT on medium-low speed until the egg whites begin to foam, about 1 minute. Crank up the speed to high and BEAT until stiff peaks form.

3. To the other large bowl, add the cake and pastry flour, white sugar, baking powder and salt. Using the whisk, WHISK until everything is combined.

4. Using the big spoon, dig a hole (about the size of a tennis ball) in the center of the flour mixture. This hole is called a well! To the well, add the egg yolks, water, vegetable oil and vanilla extract. Using the whisk, WHISK until everything is combined.

5. Using the big spoon, scoop a spoonful of batter into the bowl with the egg whites. Using the spatula, FOLD the batter into the egg whites. Repeat until all the cake batter has been added and folded into the egg whites. Go slow! You want the egg whites to stay nice and fluffy!

6. To the small bowl, add the mini chocolate chips, mini peanut butter chips and all-purpose flour. Stir with the big spoon until the mini chips are lightly dusted with flour. This will keep them from sinking to the bottom of the cake!

7. Sprinkle the mini chips into the bowl with the cake batter. Using the mixing spoon, gently MIX the chips into the batter.

8. Gently scoop the cake batter into the ungreased tube pan.

9. FIND YOUR PERSON Bake the cake until a wooden skewer stuck into the middle of the cake comes out clean, about 55–60 minutes.

10. FIND YOUR PERSON Using the oven mitts, carefully remove the cake pan from the oven and flip it upside down on a cooling rack. Let the cake cool completely upside down in the pan.

11. Once cooled, flip the cake back over. Run the tip of the butter knife between the edge of the pan and the cake to help get it out. Chip, chip, hooray!

*Save for later?* Store the cake in an airtight container for up to 2 days.

Continue your baking adventure in **Wonderpark** at **Glazes and More** (page 116)! There you can try making a fabulous glaze to deck this cake with. Our favorite flavor match is **Chocolate Shine Glaze** (page 121) . . . topped with **Chocolate Potato Chips and Pretzels** (page 133), YUM!

# Lemony Olive Oil Cake

## Makes 1 × 2-tiered cake

What do you do when life gives you lemons? Make lemon cake! This cake is super moist (from the olive oil) and has just the right amount of lemon flavor. You'll pucker up for more!

 Get Ready...

## TOOLS

- ☐ Measuring cups and spoons
- ☐ 2 x 8-inch round cake pans
- ☐ Parchment paper
- ☐ Medium bowl
- ☐ Whisk
- ☐ Large bowl
- ☐ Electric mixer
- ☐ Spatula
- ☐ Toothpicks
- ☐ Oven mitts
- ☐ Cooling racks

**There's more to explore!**
Go to the **Information Booth** on page 7 to discover more about preparing your pans.

## INGREDIENTS

| | |
|---|---|
| Cooking spray, for greasing pans | |
| 1½ cups | all-purpose flour |
| ½ cup | cake and pastry flour |
| 2 cups | white sugar |
| ½ teaspoon | table salt |
| 1 teaspoon | baking powder |
| ½ teaspoon | baking soda |
| 3 | large eggs |
| 1¼ cups | whole milk |
| 1 cup | olive oil |
| 1 tablespoon | freshly squeezed lemon juice |
| Zest from 1 lemon | |

# . . . BAKE!

1. Preheat your oven to 325°F. Cover the bottom of the cake pans with parchment paper circles. Spray the parchment paper and sides of the pans with the cooking spray.

2. To the medium bowl, add the all-purpose flour, cake and pastry flour, white sugar, salt, baking powder and baking soda. Using the whisk, WHISK until the mixture is lump-free. Set this bowl to the side.

3. To the large bowl, add the eggs, milk, olive oil, lemon juice and lemon zest. Using the electric mixer, BEAT on low speed until everything is combined.

4. Add the flour mixture to the large bowl with the oil mixture. BEAT on low speed until everything comes together. Don't overbeat this mixture.

5. Add the batter evenly to the cake pans. Using the spatula, SCRAPE down the sides and bottom of the bowl.

6. FIND YOUR PERSON Bake both cakes until a toothpick stuck in the middle of a cake comes out clean, about 35–40 minutes.

7. FIND YOUR PERSON Using the oven mitts, carefully remove the cake pans from the oven and place them on the cooling racks. Let the cakes cool completely in the pans before removing them. Remember to remove the parchment paper if it's stuck to their bottoms!

Save for later? Store the cake in an airtight container for up to 4 days.

Continue your baking adventure in **Wonderpark** at the **Fillings** (page 84) and **Frostings** (page 102). Our favorite flavor matches are **Bonjour! Pastry Cream** (page 89) for filling, and **Fluffy Cream Cheese Frosting** (page 111) colored yellow for frosting. Then topped with yellow and white sprinkles.

Fluffy Cream
Cheese Frosting
(page 111)

Bonjour! Pastry
Cream
(page 89)

SWEET

# THE GIFT SHOP

Don't leave Wonderland without visiting the Gift Shop! Here you can find all sorts of goodies about baking! First check out our Wonder-ware, a list of all of the tools we use in our recipes and what they do! And be sure to browse the Wonderland Pant-Tree to learn more about the many different ingredients found in our recipes!

# Wonder-ware!

Here's a helpful list of the baking tools used in this book and tips on how to use them!

## MEASURING

**Measuring cups and spoons:** These are what you use to measure out how much of each ingredient you need for a recipe.

**Spouted measuring cup:** This is great for measuring wet ingredients and pouring wet batters into muffin pans. When you need to move wet ingredients from one place to another, the spout lets you pour without little drips or slips! Some jobs are bigger than others so it's good to have more than one size.

## MIXING

**Mixing bowls:** These are what you use to put your ingredients into so you can mix them together. It's helpful to have three different sizes. Mixing bowls are made from all different types of materials. We recommend having both microwave-safe bowls and stainless steel bowls.

**Mixing spoon:** The spoon is said to have been around since 1000 BC. That makes it the dinosaur of kitchen tools. This is the awesome tool that you use to MIX your mixtures. Discover more on page 10.

**Whisk:** This wire tool is excellent for when you need to WHISK your ingredients together, especially if they're runny. Discover more on page 10.

**Spatula:** This is what you use to SCRAPE or FOLD. Discover more on page 10. It's good to have lots of these in different sizes.

**Electric mixer:** This is what you use to BEAT your ingredients together when you need more speed than a whisk. Discover more on page 11.

**Stand mixer:** This is an awesome tool because it can mix *a lot* of ingredients in its big ol' bowl for a long time. It sits right on your counter and comes in all sorts of fun colors. For our Poop Cookies (page 47), a stand mixer is a must!

**Blender**: Great for mixing liquid ingredients and mush'n' things fast! Always make sure your blender is turned off before you plug it in! Its blades are sharp so always check in with YOUR PERSON before using.

**Food processor**: This handy gadget is great for chopping up ingredients like dried fruit or nuts. Its blades are sharp so always check in with YOUR PERSON before using.

## POTS, PANS AND SHEETS

**Saucepan**: A good saucepan, ideally with a spout, is a baker's best friend. You can use it to warm milk, melt chocolate and reduce fruit. A spout makes pouring hot liquids a snap!

**Pots**: Pots rock for boiling water and for cooking larger recipes like our FUN-dant (page 130) as they come in big sizes.

**Cookie sheet**: These rectangular flat metal sheets are what you bake cookies on. Most of our cookie recipes make more cookies than fit on one sheet, so it's a good idea to have two.

**Cake pans**: These shallow, round metal pans are what you use for baking cakes in. We like 8-inch and 9-inch pans.

**Muffin pans**: This 12-cup baking pan is what you use to bake cupcakes in. Most of our cupcake recipes make at least 18 cupcakes, so it's a good idea to have two pans!

**Donut pan**: These are what you use to make round-looking donuts. Do-nut forget to grease them—donut batter likes to stick. Most of our donut recipes make 18 donuts, so it's a good idea to have two or three pans.

**Loaf pan**: This rectangular metal pan is awesome for baking sweet breads and loaves—and for freezing our Vanilla Ice Scream (page 100) in! We loaf you, loaf pan!

**Tube cake pan**: This pan is totally tubular! It's shaped like an inner tube that you'd find in a water park and is used to bake fluffy cakes that like to rise up tall!

## KEEPING THINGS COLD

**Freezer**: The freezer can be as important to a baker as the oven when it comes to cakes! Not only does this ice box keep baked goods fresh, it also makes frosting a snap, as a cake is less crumbly when the layers are frozen. Discover more on page 30.

**Fridge**: This happy place keeps all your food fresh and chilled. We often use the fridge to cool batters or doughs before baking or to firm up fillings and frostings. And, of course, we go to it for snacks!

## GETTING THINGS HOT

**Oven**: This big tool is what you use to do most of your baking in. It has a range of temperatures, that can be set in either Celsius (°C) or Fahrenheit (°F). We use °F in our recipes. Hot tip: Even though it can be super tempting to peek at your baking when it's in the oven, try your best to keep the oven door closed (so the heat doesn't escape) for a nice, even bake. Always check in with YOUR PERSON before you use the oven!

Stove: This important tool has burners that heat up for cooking our ingredients. We often use the stove for cooking our fillings and melting chocolate and butter. Always check in with YOUR PERSON before you use the stove!

Microwave: This tiny oven is great for warming and melting ingredients in a jiffy. It's super important to make sure that your dish is microwave-safe before you put it in the microwave! No metals or soft plastics, please!

Oven mitts: A good pair of fitted oven mitts is an absolute must when you're using the oven or stove. We love using mitts with silicone patterns on the hands for extra grip!

## TIMING, TESTING AND COOLING

Kitchen timer: What time is it? Time to get a kitchen timer! A clock that works as a timer is a super-important tool in the kitchen. Set it to keep track of how long your goodies have been baking!

Toothpicks: These are our preferred and safest way to check that our baking is done! Carefully stick a clean toothpick in the center of a baked good. If it comes out without any goo on it, you know that your baking is finished cooking! Toothpicks are also very handy for adding food

coloring gel to your baking. For taller cakes, like our Chipper Chocolate Chip Cake (page 189), we use longer wooden skewers.

Cooling racks: Use these to place your hot cookie sheets on when they come out of the oven so your goodies can cool. They also come in handy when it's time to glaze your baked goods.

## DECORATING

Piping bag with coupler: A piping bag is a triangle-shaped bag usually made out of plastic or silicone that you scoop frosting into. The coupler is a piece of hard plastic that you attach on the end of the bag to hold the piping tip in place. Discover more on page 34.

Piping tips: Piping tips are the pointy ends you attach to the narrow end of the piping bag. They come in all different shapes and sizes, so each one makes a different pattern! Be our guest at the Piping Party (page 32) to discover everything you need to know about piping!

Offset spatula: It might be called an OFFset spatula, but this handy tool is bang-ON for frosting cakes. And its flat edge makes lifting cookies off surfaces a breeze!

## OTHER WONDERFUL TOOLS

Sifter: This fun tool is awesome for getting rid of bumps and lumps in any of your ingredients. Simply place the sifter on top of a bowl and dump your ingredients into it. Lightly shake the sifter. Your ingredients will fall through the holes of the sifter, lump-free.

**Box grater**: Say "cheese"! We like using a boxed cheese grater to zest our citrus fruit. It's super easy to use. Just run your fruit down the small-toothed side of the grater. Stop when you see the white part (pith) of the fruit. You don't want

The pith is pery pitter

that in your baking! Need room-temperature butter quickly? Grate your cold butter down the big-toothed side of the box grater, like you would cheese. Wait a couple of minutes and your butter shavings will be at room temperature!

**Vegetable peeler**: Move over, carrots. We love to use this tiny handheld tool for making chocolate curls! Discover more on page 138.

**Cookie cutters**: It's always fun to have these in your drawer for when you make our Sugar Sugar

Sugar Cookies (page 59) or for cutting out some donuts (page 158). They come in all shapes and sizes. Have fun collecting them!

**Cupcake liners**: We like lining our pans with these paper cups for easy cupcake removal—plus they're great for catching the crumbs when you're eating them!

**Silicone baking mats**: We like lining our cookie sheets with these mats. They are reusable and have tiny built-in grips so cookies spread less when baking. These mats are also great for rolling out dough, catching spills and eating your lunch on!

**Pastry brush**: This is like a paintbrush for baking! It's great for spreading out ingredients in a nice thin layer and for dipping into coconut oil to grease your baking pans. Don't have a pastry brush? Try using a toothbrush—a new one!

**Rolling pin**: Rolling pins are long cylinders that you roll over dough to make it nice and flat. For the best, un-stickiest results, we always recommend rolling on a smooth surface, and placing a piece of parchment paper between your dough and your rolling pin.

**Scissors**: It's always handy to have a pair of scissors in the kitchen! They're a great tool for snipping piping bags and cutting fruit and candies.

**Big spoon, fork and butter knife**: These utensils aren't just for taste testing! They are useful in baking for scooping, stirring and slicing ingredients.

# Wonderland Pant-Tree

Thanks for visiting our pantry! Here you can find everything you need to know about the ingredients we use to make our desserts!

## FLOUR

This fine powdery ingredient is the key to making most baked goods. It's what you get when you grind up grains really, really small. There are many types of flours that belong in the flour family and they all do awesome things. Check them out below!

**All-purpose flour**: You can probably find this flour in your cupboard now. All-purpose flour (sometimes shortened to "AP flour") is the most popular of all the flours because it's super-duper easy to bake with. Like its name suggests, it can handle most jobs. AP flour comes in bleached and unbleached, both work great for the recipes in this book.

**Cake and pastry flour**: This is the lightest flour in the flour family. It's made up of less protein and gluten than all-purpose flour, so it creates tender, fluffier baked goods. We love cake and pastry flour for our cupcakes. If you don't have cake and pastry flour, you can make your own by adding

1 tablespoon of cornstarch to every 1 cup of all-purpose flour. Now that's flour power!

**Gluten-free flour**: This flour is made by grinding up different varieties of seeds, nuts, roots, beans and gluten-free grains. (Gluten is a protein that comes from wheat and can give some people bad allergic reactions and bellyaches! Not fun!) Our go-to gluten-free flour is a 1:1 baking flour.

## BAKING POWDER

Or maybe we should call it baking POWER! This white powder is what lightens and lifts your cakes, cupcakes, donuts and cookies. Baking powder contains baking soda and cornstarch. It will lift your baked goods sky-high!

## BAKING SODA

Baking soda is also used to make your baking fluffy. It has a high pH level and will react to lemons, vinegars and heat by creating bubbles that will make your baking blast off!

## SALT

Pass the salt, please! This humble ingredient is key to making your flavors pop and balancing the sweetness in your baking.

**Table salt**: Table salt is preferred in most baking because it dissolves completely when it's heated.

**Sea salt**: This salt is made from evaporated salt water from oceans or salt lakes, and is absolutely delicious sprinkled on our Chocolate Fudge Cookies (page 57).

## OIL

Oil comes in lots of types that are great for baking: olive, canola, vegetable and coconut. Oil gives your baking moisture and contains no water, so it won't evaporate in the oven. Your cakes and cupcakes will be so moist!

**Cooking spray**: Cooking spray is cooking oil that comes in a canister with a nozzle. We use cooking spray to coat our cupcake liners and baking pans so our baking doesn't stick. You can find it in lots of types of oils: canola, vegetable, sunflower, avocado, olive and coconut. Try your best not to use too much or your recipe will end up absorbing the flavor of the spray.

## SUGARS

**White sugar**: This is also known as granulated sugar. White sugar is the most common sugar used in baking and contains no molasses, unlike its sweeter relatives.

**Brown sugar**: Brown sugar is just white sugar with molasses in it. It gives baking a sweet, caramel flavor. Brown sugar comes in light, golden yellow and dark. For our recipes we prefer light brown sugar.

**Powdered sugar**: Powdered sugar is also known as icing sugar or confectioner's sugar. It is just finely ground white sugar that often has a bit of cornstarch in it to prevent it from clumping. It's perfect for creating fluffy frostings and silky glazes.

**Superfine sugar**: Superfine sugar is white sugar that's ground into really small pieces. It's great in baking because it dissolves quickly. If you don't have superfine sugar, you can make your own by blending white sugar in your blender for 1 minute. How super?!

## SWEETENERS

**Fancy molasses**: This super-sticky ingredient comes from sugar cane or sugar beets. It's used in baking for its rich robust flavor.

**Maple syrup**: Maple syrup comes from the maple tree. It's what you get when you boil down the sticky maple sap. This sweet amber syrup is delicious on pancakes and waffles and is also great to bake with!

**Honey**: Honey is the sticky sweet golden liquid that bees make! This natural sweetener is a great alternative to sugar in baking. You could say it's buzz-worthy!

**Caramel extract**: This has all the flavor of caramel but it's packed into a teeny-tiny bottle. Because each drop packs a big caramel-ly taste, it should be used sparingly.

**Corn syrup**: Made from the starch of corn, this thick, sticky ooey-gooey liquid comes in different colors that range in sweetness. It's not only used as a sweetener. It's also used to prevent sugar from crystallizing and sticking together in sauces or fillings.

## CHOCOLATE

**Dark chocolate**: This chocolate is the starting place for all other chocolates! It's made of mostly cocoa beans and a tiny amount of sugar. No milk found here!

**White chocolate**: White chocolate is made from milk, sugar, vanilla and cocoa butter. This luxurious ingredient is technically not considered chocolate because it doesn't have any cocoa solids in it. Imposter-chocolate!

**Milk chocolate**: Light and sweet, creamy and soft, milk chocolate gets its name because it's made with a lot of milk.

**Semisweet chocolate**: This chocolate is the perfect balance of richness, bitterness and sweetness, making it the go-to chocolate in baking. Semisweet chocolate has sugar added to its dark chocolate base.

**Cocoa powder**: This is chocolate in powdered form! Cocoa powder comes from the cacao bean—it's what's left over after the bean has been fermented and roasted. Cocoa powder comes in natural and Dutch-process types. Natural cocoa powder is lighter, fruitier and bitter, while Dutch process is darker and richer in flavor. We use natural cocoa powder in the recipes in this book.

## SPICES AND FLAVORINGS

**Vanilla extract**: We use this sweet dark liquid in a lot of our baking. It's the perfect spice to round out the overall flavors in your recipe, and it makes flavors like chocolate sing!

**Vanilla bean paste**: This thick brown paste is a combination of vanilla extract, vanilla bean

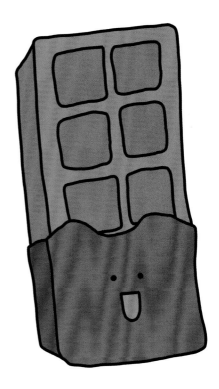

powder and flecks of vanilla seed from the vanilla pod. All that vanilla gives this paste a boost of pure, luxurious vanilla flavor.

**Banana extract**: Sometimes in baking you need an extra POW of flavor! Imagine taking the essence of a bunch of bananas and smashing it up in a little jar. BAM! You got banana extract.

**Cinnamon**: This popular spice comes in sticks or is ground into a fine brown powder. Cinnamon comes from the inner bark of the Cinnamomum tree. We use cinnamon in baking for its warm, rich taste and lovely smells. Say this five times fast: She seeks six sticks of cinnamon from the Cinnamomum tree!

**Cloves**: Cloves are dried flower buds from an evergreen tree that grows in India, Madagascar and Indonesia. This little spice packs a big punch and is often used alongside other spices, like cinnamon and nutmeg, for cozy fall and winter baking.

**Nutmeg**: Ground from the seeds of the nutmeg tree, this spice is warm and nutty. We like using just a pinch in our baking, as a little goes a long way.

Mmmm . . .

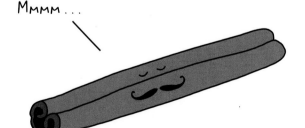

**Cardamom**: This spice comes from the ginger family. When ground, it has a citrusy, warm flavor that's excellent in baking.

## DAIRY AND EGGS

**Butter**: No wonder Betty bought a bit of butter! This rich and creamy ingredient is made by churning the cream from cow's milk. It comes salted or unsalted. We like baking with salted butter because it brings out all the flavors in the recipe. Betty says, "Boo-ya!"

**Vegan butter**: This plant-based butter is made without dairy! It's created by combining plants like avocado or coconut with olive oil and water.

**Whole milk**: Whole milk is the milk that comes right out of the cow. It is very rich in milk fat, so it's got a big bold milky flavor and body.

**Dairy-free milk**: Almond, cashew, oat, rice, soy, coconut . . . there are so many great dairy-free milks to choose from! These milks are often made by soaking the ingredient in water and then blending and straining. Each milk has a unique flavor and texture, and they're all a great choice for vegan baking.

**Coconut cream**: Coconut cream is a thicker version of coconut milk. It has more coconut than water so it's great for adding richness and flavor to your vegan baking.

**Whipping cream**: This is perfect for creating delicious fluffy whipped creamy clouds, or whipping up to create airy dessert toppings!

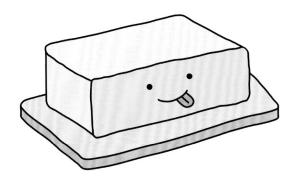

Whipping cream contains A LOT of milk fat and is heavenly for heating.

**Table cream**: Somewhere in the middle of all the creams is table cream. Table cream is great for baking because it adds richness but doesn't have enough fat to whip up like its cousin Whipping Cream.

**Buttermilk**: This is the tangy liquid you get when you churn butter. Buttermilk is high in acidity, so it naturally softens your baked goods, making them tender and moist. TIP: If you don't have buttermilk, you can make your own by adding 1 tablespoon of lemon juice to 1 cup of whole milk and leaving it on the counter for 5–10 minutes.

**Milk powder**: No straws needed here! Milk powder is milk that's been dried and crushed into a powder. We use this ingredient to add an extra-creamy milky flavor to some of our recipes!

**Sour cream**: Like its name suggests, sour cream is regular cream that's been soured. It is super thick and has a ton of flavor, so it's great for adding moisture and tartness to cakes and baked goods.

**Cream cheese**: Cream cheese is a soft, spreadable, mild-tasting cheese made from milk and cream. We love using cream cheese in our frostings for that little tangy taste of heaven!

**Eggs**: Eggs are a great source of protein and are used in baking for so many reasons: they hold all the other ingredients together, provide lift when beaten, can thicken sauces and creams and give your baking moisture. TIP: When you're using eggs, get into the habit of cracking them first into a small bowl of their own before adding them to your baking. This will make it easy to pick out any pesky shells that might have fallen in when the egg was cracked. Now get crackin'!

## FRUIT, FRUIT JUICE AND DRIED FRUIT

**Applesauce**: This naturally sweet sauce comes from cooking apples down until they're mushy and then blending them. We use applesauce in baking to sweeten and add moisture to our baked goods. In vegan baking, applesauce can sometimes be used instead of eggs.

**Strawberries**: Great for baking with, this teardrop-shaped red berry ranges from tart to sweet depending on size and color.

**Blueberries**: This berry should be wearing a cape because it's a superfood! This small, round blue berry is jam-packed with vitamins, jam-packed with minerals and great packed in our jam!

**Banana**: Bananas are an amazing fruit! Not only are they packed with potassium and nutrients, but they also add moisture and great flavor to your baking. Did you know that bananas grow upside down? And that a single banana is called a finger and a bunch of bananas is called a hand? Now that's a hand we want to shake!

**Cherries**: This teeny, tiny, ruby-red stone fruit grows on trees! We love using cherries in baking because they can add a nice balance of tartness and sweetness to our baked goods.

**Orange juice**: The juice from an orange! This citrus fruit adds a great zip and moisture to your baking.

**Lemon juice**: Lemon juice is the juice you get from a lemon. This pale yellow citrus is excellent for adding a zing to your baking. For the best lemony flavor, roll the lemon on the counter a few times to loosen up the fruit before juicing. Zing!

**Lemon zest**: Lemon zest is the little flakes of lemon peel that you get when you grate the outside of a lemon. Lemon zest is PACKED with lemon flavor and adds a real zippiness and brightness to batters, sugar and frostings. Be careful not to include the white part of the peel. It's very bitter!

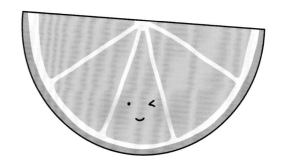

**Dates**: This fruit comes from the palm tree and grows in bundles. Dates belong to the stone fruit family—just like peaches, mangoes and cherries—and are great for adding sweetness and texture to baking.

**Coconut flakes**: Sweetened or unsweetened, coconut flakes are shredded from a coconut and then dried. Use them to top a donut or a cake.

## OTHER WONDERFUL INGREDIENTS

**Distilled white vinegar**: This common clear vinegar is a great ingredient in baking because it helps baking rise and keeps it moist and airy. This mild acid also enhances the flavor of your other ingredients. When you're using any type of vinegar in baking, remember that a little goes a long way!

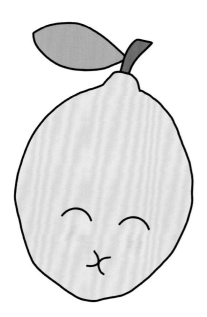

**Cream of tartar**: HELP! We need help in the kitchen! Call Cream of Tartar! This magical white powder helps firm up egg whites, gives baked goods a fluffy lift and prevents sugars from sticking together when you really don't want them to.

**Coffee**: Good morning, taste buds! We use coffee in our baking to bring out the deep rich flavors of chocolate. This dark brown drink contains caffeine, so use it sparingly.

**Food coloring liquid**: This is paint for your food! Food coloring liquid is made of edible synthetic color and water. It comes in all sorts of colors and it's great for coloring frostings and glazes.

**Food coloring gel**: Like food coloring liquid, this is also paint for your food! But this paint is made out of edible synthetic color and corn syrup or glycerin. It's thicker than its liquid cousin, and it packs more color. Food coloring gel is great for coloring batters and doughs because it stays bright when you bake it.

**Yeast**: Yeast is a living thing! A teeny-tiny hungry organism that has its own unique smell and flavor. It is used in doughs for breads, pizzas, soft pretzels and some donuts. Like any living thing, yeast needs food to survive. It likes to eat sugar, and when it does, it produces gas bubbles! These bubbles are what makes our doughs rise up high. BRRFT . . . Excuse you, Yeast!

**Gelatin**: Gelatin is a gummy, sticky protein that comes from animals (so vegetarians and vegans beware!). We sometimes use gelatin in baking to thicken fillings like our Princess Banana Lips (page 98).

**Cornstarch**: Don't be so corny, it's just starch! Cornstarch is the starch found in corn. This fine white powder is used in baking to thicken fillings, puddings and sauces.

**Sweetened condensed milk**: Squished milk! Sweetened condensed milk is cow's milk where the water has been removed and, in most cases, replaced by sugar. It's great for making fudge and candies, and we love using it in our Vanilla Ice Scream (page 100). AAAAAAAGGGHHHHHHH!

**Vegan marshmallows**: Made from plant-based ingredients like tapioca starch and cane sugar, these soft plant-based marshmallows are the perfect ingredient to give our vegan frosting structure.

**Jelly powder**: This crystallized fruity powder is great in baking because it gives a boost of flavor and a pop of color to frostings and batters. It can also be used to firm up recipes as well because it contains gelatin.

**Peanut butter**: Did you know peanut butter doesn't have any butter in it? It's made by dry-roasting peanuts and grinding them into a paste. You can buy peanut butter sweetened or natural (that means there's nothing in it but nuts). Either way, this lip-smacking spread is high in protein and jam-packed with nutty flavor, and comes in crunchy and smooth textures.

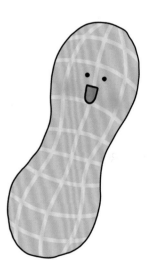

# Thank You

Baking is love. Which is why we first want to thank our families, every single one of you.

Our children, Harlow, Jack and Charlie. You three are Baking Wonderland's first adventurers. We made you eat cake for breakfast! And we'll do it again! Your imagination and creativity constantly inspire us. Thank you for being you.

Craig and John, thank you for the million little things you do every day to make this life so good and full. Thank you to our unofficial copy editors, Mom and Stewart. Our sister, Britt, and partner, Jory, and our nephew (and biggest fan), Jasper Nash. Thank you for being our sounding board, for believing in us, for scouring our freezers for baked goods (which we all know taste amazing frozen!).

Thank you to our girlfriends, our pack. Thank you for always lifting us up and encouraging us to keep going.

Thank you to Robert McCullough for giving us a pony! We didn't really get a pony, but your kindness and encouragement made us feel like we did! And you gave us Lindsay Paterson! Our incredible editor who let us lean in really close during meetings and who laughed with us and dreamed with us. Your talent and vision helped make Baking Wonderland a real place! Thank you to Marian Staresinic. You're like the best jam in a peanut butter and jam sandwich—you brought us all together!

Big thanks to our copy editor, Lesley Cameron, for your careful work. Without you this book would have triple the number of exclamation marks!! We like them a lot!!!

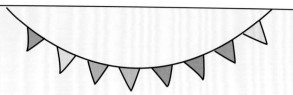

Thank you to the female powerhouse that is our creative team: our photographer, Reena Newman, and food stylist, Sage Dakota. Thank you for bringing your talent and enthusiasm to Wonderland! Thank you to our illustrator, Angela Choa. Your bright energy and zest for life spill from your work! Special thanks to Monica Smiley for your illustration of us. And thank you to our designer, Emma Dolan. You're a creative wizard with an impeccable eye who put this magic together!

Big thanks to Walter Vaz for lending us a kitchen to play in. We are forever grateful for your generosity.

Helen Tansey, you are the special ingredient everyone needs. Thank you for making us feel beautiful, supported and loved—in photographs and in life.

Enormous thanks to our recipe testers and kid-baker-extraordinaires: Emily, Laura, Finn, Harper, Ember, Brody, Gracen, Maddox-Louise, Eli, Ezra and Hannah. (And their people, our friends and family who probably had to do a lot of dishes afterward!)

And lastly, thank you, reader, for coming along on this baking adventure with us. We hope we're giving you a beginning, much like our mom did for us . . . We can't wait to see where you go from here.

Love, Jean and Rachel

# Index

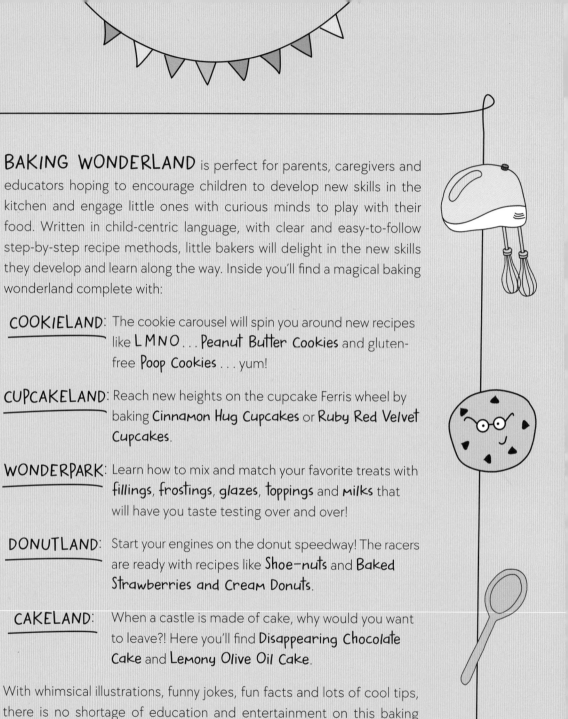

**BAKING WONDERLAND** is perfect for parents, caregivers and educators hoping to encourage children to develop new skills in the kitchen and engage little ones with curious minds to play with their food. Written in child-centric language, with clear and easy-to-follow step-by-step recipe methods, little bakers will delight in the new skills they develop and learn along the way. Inside you'll find a magical baking wonderland complete with:

**COOKIELAND**: The cookie carousel will spin you around new recipes like L M N O . . . Peanut Butter Cookies and gluten-free Poop Cookies . . . yum!

**CUPCAKELAND**: Reach new heights on the cupcake Ferris wheel by baking Cinnamon Hug Cupcakes or Ruby Red Velvet Cupcakes.

**WONDERPARK**: Learn how to mix and match your favorite treats with fillings, frostings, glazes, toppings and milks that will have you taste testing over and over!

**DONUTLAND**: Start your engines on the donut speedway! The racers are ready with recipes like Shoe-nuts and Baked Strawberries and Cream Donuts.

**CAKELAND**: When a castle is made of cake, why would you want to leave?! Here you'll find Disappearing Chocolate Cake and Lemony Olive Oil Cake.

With whimsical illustrations, funny jokes, fun facts and lots of cool tips, there is no shortage of education and entertainment on this baking adventure.

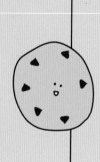